"The first few weeks of living [...] be a make or break time. Larry and Susan identify many important adjustments in *First 30 Daze* that will help you not just 'make it,' but thrive from day one."
—DALE LOSCH, president of Crossworld, author of *A Better Way: Make Disciples Wherever Life Happens*

"Perhaps the most difficult part of transitioning to life and ministry in a new country is knowing where to start. Larry and Susan provide a survival guide and roadmap for navigating the make-or-break first month in a new place. Part memoir, part practical how-to, *First 30 Daze* introduces readers to simple, easy-to-implement activities that will make the transition a smooth one."
—CALEB CRIDER, co-author of *Tradecraft: For The Church On Mission*; contributing author, *Whom Shall We Send?*; co-founder of The Upstream Collective; lead instructional design, IMB

"What a profoundly simple yet insightfully written book! I love the down-to-earth style and questions, the encouraging spirit, and the challenging use of Scripture. So much so, I find my heart wishing that I could personally go to a new culture again!"
—BUD FRAY, author of *Both Feet In* and *It is Enough*

"Having experienced the transition into multiple different cultures themselves, Larry and Susan McCrary provide an invaluable resource to those following God's call into a new country. As a pastor, I am eager to place *First 30 Daze* into the hands of students studying abroad, teachers, marketplace workers, and all those we're sending to the nations."
—JASON HAYES, author of *Blemished: How the Message of Malachi Confronts Empty Religion* and *Follow Me*; co-author of *Lost and Found: The Younger Unchurched and the Churches that Reach Them*; lead pastor of Shoreline Church, Knoxville, Tennessee

"What a resource! Larry and Susan's wealth of personal experiences overseas and their wisdom gained through years of helping others thrive in a cross-cultural environment come through right from the very first pages. Whether you want to know how to pray for your missionary friends as they transition overseas or you are preparing for an international move yourself, I enthusiastically recommend *First 30 Daze*."
  —JOSH MCQUAID, director of organizational engagement, TEAM

"*First 30 Daze* is a fantastic resource for those transitioning to cross-cultural situations. Through the Word of God and their personal experiences, the McCrarys provide a guide to help people be humble, intentional, and grounded in the midst of these transitions. May God get the glory as His followers move throughout the nations and live this out."
  —MELODY HARPER, Global Studies department chair and assistant professor, Liberty University

"*First 30 Daze* is one of the most practical guides for being on mission in a new place and goes beyond theory to the daily practices that will help students, professionals, and others transition well into a new culture. I highly recommend this healthy, biblical, and down-to-earth guide."
  —CHAD STILLWELL, IMB student mobilization leader

First 30 Daze

First 30 Daze

Practical Encouragement
for Living Abroad Intentionally

Larry and Susan McCrary

UPSTREAM

Louisville, Kentucky

Printed in the United States of America.

ISBN 978-0-9961847-1-7

This title also is available as an eBook (ISBN 978-0-9961847-2-4).

The Upstream Collective
P. O. Box 23871
Knoxville, TN 37933

Editor: Kim P. Davis
Cover and interior designer: Rachel Allen
Author cover photo: Melissa Hill Photography

Dedication

To the thousands of
Christ followers who find themselves
in a new city and culture,
desiring to be salt and light

"In the same way, let your light shine before others,
so that they may see your good works and give glory to your
Father who is in heaven."

Matthew 5:16

CONTENTS

CONTENTS

Acknowledgments

We want to thank our two wonderful children, Megan and Parker, who have blessed us in so many ways and have been, and continue to be, with us on the journey.

We could not have completed this project without the provision of a mountain getaway in North Carolina. Thanks, David and Laura. We already are thinking about our next writing project.

We are thankful for several friends who helped us think, tweak, and edit: Tep Lim, Allison, Abigail Ramsey, Claire Flippin, Nicole Wanke, and Andrea Hayes. So grateful for your wonderful advice and your treasured friendship!

Many thanks to our final editor, Kim P. Davis. Her ability to see this book for what it is meant to be means the world to us.

We are thankful for Rachel Allen for designing our book and making this a useful field guide.

And of course, thanks to our publisher, The Upstream Collective. Always indebted to our team and the Stream!

Foreword

One of the greatest blessings that God can allow a family or a single is the joy of moving to a new country with a different culture. Yet, the thought of moving terrifies the hearts of many. Relocating for missional reasons is one of the central themes of the Bible. Historically from Abraham to Jesus, when "the Word became flesh and dwelt among us" (John1:14), God has communicated the importance of being sent for a purpose. His love was transferred to us in the ultimate way through the incarnation, when God became man.

When faced with an opportunity to move to a new country, we can view it as a nightmare or as an adventure. Most days we get to choose! Living in an unfamiliar place can be your opportunity to be Christ to people who have never known eternal love.

After 30 moves, four languages, and 32 years, our family has experienced all the ups and downs of living internationally. Some places were responsive to the gospel of Jesus Christ, and other places were hostile. Some moves were to first-world settings filled with churches and shopping centers, while others were, in the words of one Somali man, "no longer a third-world country but a pre-world country." In these places, expatriates often have no place to pray and no place to play. Creating a place to be with God and with each other in a new country will be a daily challenge in the beginning. *First 30 Daze* offers a way to thrive, no matter where God sends us, so that we can take advantage of the opportunities living internationally brings. Whether it's shopping at an internationally known furniture store or having a locally skilled woodworker make one's furniture, our goal remains the same. Learn to laugh at yourself, see beauty in all of God's children, and truly be "at home" wherever God might plant you.

Years ago, my wife and I were given great advice when forced out of Malawi due to repeated bouts of malaria. A wise leader said, "Serving God is not a matter of location, it's a matter of obedience." Being obedient to serve Jesus, while living internationally, keeps us on task until our hearts catch up to where God has sent us.

Nik Ripken,

author of *The Insanity of God* and *The Insanity of Obedience*

Introduction

Some people say it is not how you start but how you finish. I have heard this statement in a variety of situations, but it is well exemplified in the sport of running. In my case, perhaps jogging is a better description!

One time while participating in a 5K race, I made two mistakes. The first mistake was running with a guy who is fast and in great shape. The second mistake was running with a guy bent on being at the starting line with the lead pack who actually run rather than jog. We took off as the gun sounded, and I ran my personal best for the first kilometer. The next two kilometers were even better, because we ran downhill. By the time we completed kilometer three, my friend was out of sight, but I was having the race of my life. Just when I thought it was easier than expected, reality presented itself. The route started its uphill climb. No longer did I enjoy the race, and the fourth and fifth kilometers were two of the slowest kilometers I ever recorded. I did finish, but I felt like Jell-o. It took extreme effort to cross the finish line.

The valuable lesson I learned is that it's important how one starts. The pace I set in the 5K was not sustainable. In fact, it was not even close to a sustainable pace for me—ever! In races since then, I do much better when I start at a good pace and as the race progresses, I have more to give at the end. This strategy leaves more energy for the hills.

I think this strategy also is true in many things we do in life. How you start is extremely important when it comes to moving to a different city in another country.

First 30 Daze will attempt to help as you start a new venture during an overwhelming and daze-like time. Each day of the first 30 days in your new country, applicable topics will be introduced to make your transition smoother. Beginning the day you arrive isn't obligatory, but starting soon after arriving will definitely increase your chances of starting well. Perhaps if you are with your family or even a friend, you can discuss and put into practice these suggestions.

Being a part of a non-profit sector allows us to live in and travel to many cities in the United States, as well as in Europe. As followers of Jesus, wherever we live or travel, our goal is to live out our faith in a different culture. It does not matter if you are a full-time vocational Christian worker, an international company employee, a student studying abroad, or a person who simply wants to live and work in another country—the first 30 days matter! The sooner that you can get out the door, learn the culture, meet people, build relationships, and discover what God has in store for you, the sooner you will feel at home and love your new environment.

Thirty topics and Scripture verses are introduced as well as practical ways to apply what you've learned each day through a simple but fun application assignment.

You may want to use the book as an individual devotional, with your family, or with a group. Regardless, it is short and practical so that you have plenty of time to get out and enjoy your new home.

Larry and Susan McCrary

FIRST 30 DAZE • FIRST 30 DAZE

DAY# 1

HUMILITY

Day 1: Humility

"Then King David went in and sat before the LORD and said, 'Who am I, O Lord GOD, and what is my house, that you have brought me thus far? And yet this was a small thing in your eyes, O Lord GOD. You have spoken also of your servant's house for a great while to come, and this is instruction for mankind, O Lord GOD! And what more can David say to you? For you know your servant, O Lord GOD! Because of your promise, and according to your own heart, you have brought about all this greatness, to make your servant know it. Therefore you are great, O LORD God. For there is none like you, and there is no God besides you, according to all that we have heard with our ears.'"

2 Samuel 7:18-22

Day 1: Humility

There is no better time to practice humility than when you are living outside of your comfort zone. Moving abroad provides the opportunity to experience humility on a broad scale. Although I could mention many times when we faced shortcomings, communicating in the heart language is one of many ways we adopted a posture of humility.

Early in our time in Spain, my wife, Susan, tried to express to our language teacher something embarrassing that happened while in the community, but instead of using the word for embarrass, she told the teacher that she was pregnant! Another time, she and our children went into a pet store. A cute bunny caught their attention, but when she asked the store employee about the rabbit, Susan called it a crab. Even our children corrected her mistake, to their and her dismay! It's rough when small children pick up a new language before the parents! I won't even mention my many language faux pas, but let's just say there are some I probably shouldn't tell you!

 Human nature has a funny way of combating the discomfort of being brought low by making us exert ourselves all the harder to prove our worth. That's when the age-old sin of pride enters. When we feel inadequate or inept, we sense the need to show others and ourselves that we aren't deficient. It takes a great deal of fighting this urge to put oneself in an attitude of true humility.

Entering a new culture requires a humble spirit. You are a guest in this new place. The people around you know a thing or two (or more!) about their own culture. Trust them. Lean on them. Be willing to admit you don't know much but are willing and eager to learn. People are gracious and want to help, especially when they see your sincerity in immersing yourself into their world.

Humility must be genuine. People can sense a fake ten miles away! Humility starts with the correct view of self before the Lord. Knowing who He is and how great, awesome, and mighty He is puts us in the proper position before Him—on our knees. We realize that He knows and cares about us, because He has created and loves us.

In talking with a friend about humility, she pointed me to the story of David in 2 Samuel 7:18 -22. David had an attitude of humility before the Lord. He basically said in this passage that he was nothing compared to the greatness of God. Submitting to God and acknowledging who He is leads us to praise Him and give Him the glory He deserves and requires. By acknowledging His greatness and His love for us when we don't deserve it, we begin to see others around us through His eyes and with His love. We want others to know how awesome God is, too. When we surrender to His will for us, we are ready to humbly say, "I am His, and whatever He desires for me is what I want."

> Entering a new culture requires a humble spirit.

God is our strength. Be willing to submit to His guidance for everything. This attitude of humility will serve you well in your journey of faith, as well as in the journey in a new place. Start your day with a prayer for humility. Acknowledge who God is and ask for His power and strength to guide you. Humble men and women aren't self-absorbed. An outward and upward focus goes a long way in having a humble spirit.

Day 1: Application

Today as you go into your new location, concentrate on looking outward and upward. Space is provided for you to journal your thoughts below.

 Outward focus: What do you imagine are the needs of the people around you? Do they have evident physical needs? Emotional needs? Imminent and critical needs? Or do they not seem to have any needs at all? What are hidden needs that they may have?

 Upward focus: Thank God for the people in your community. Pray specifically for the door attendant at your apartment, the postal service clerk, the sales associate, the shop owner, the neighbor, the teacher, students, or others. You may not know their needs, but our heavenly Father knows and cares for them. Pray that they may seek Him and find Him.

FIRST 30 DAZE • FIRST 30 DAZE

DAY# 1

JOURNAL

 Who did you meet?

 What did you eat?

 Where did you visit?

Did you learn anything new about
the culture?

 Did you have any language or
cultural mishaps?

TAKE A FEW MINUTES TO WRITE DOWN
SOME TAKEAWAYS FROM YOUR DAY.

JOURNAL ENTRY
DAY 1
1
DAY 1
JOURNAL ENTRY

Day 2: Smile!

"But the fruit of the Spirit is love, joy, peace, patience, kindness, goodness, faithfulness, gentleness, self-control ..."

Galatians 5:22-23

Day 2: Smile!

When we prepared for our first move overseas, our children were five and nine years old. My wife traveled abroad as a child, but I had not. Certainly neither of us had lived in another country. We soon found out that being a tourist and actually living abroad are two totally different things.

Moving to Spain, we decided to make a verbal family pact. It was never in writing or posted on the refrigerator, but we determined to consistently follow three goals: be humble, learn the language, and smile.

The first goal, humility, comes as a daily dose of reality when living abroad. There is nothing like a brand new place, culture, and people to make uncomfortable situations the new norm. Vulnerability is something most people try to avoid but to live abroad and do it well, you have to take risks and be OK when you make mistakes. Not being in control of circumstances gives opportunities for personal growth, if an attitude of humility is employed to create an environment for learning.

> ...a smile can bridge differences.

Acquiring the language, our second goal, is key to building relationships. I happen to be from East Tennessee, and sometimes I feel that English is my second language! Before leaving the States to move to Spain, the only Spanish I knew was, "¡Yo quiero Taco Bell!", a popular slogan at that time. Yes, that's right—a television commercial taught me my first Spanish phrase! Doubts aside, we dove headfirst into language learning from day one of living in our new home. It was not easy, and it was stressful, especially in the early days. However, being able to share the gospel in someone's heart language is of utmost importance to communicate His love to others.

Finally, the third goal is to smile a lot, or at least when appropriate! You may find that in some cultures, smiling at strangers is not normal. But we have found that a smile can bridge differences. As a Christ follower, the Holy Spirit dwells within you. Growing in your relationship with Christ enables you to exhibit the fruit of the Spirit, which are outward expressions of Him dwelling in you. The heart filled with love, joy, peace, patience, kindness, goodness, faithfulness, gentleness, and self-control gives reason to smile at others and at self.

Smiling opens a lot of doors for sharing the gospel. It also can bring calm to a tense situation. The act of smiling is not rocket science; it is a simple act. However, amidst culture shock and the stress of living abroad, smiling may not be an automatic response. It takes practice as you rely on the strength of the Holy Spirit to smile when you're not feeling it. Your outward expressions and body language affect how others perceive you. People can determine if you are friendly and open to conversation by observation.

Just as it's not easy some days to share a smile with others, it also is not always easy to smile at yourself. How do you learn not to take yourself so seriously? It can be hard to laugh at your mistakes and your circumstances. God wants to help you experience joy that overflows. Unfamiliar surroundings, people, and even the language barrier give plenty of opportunities to extend grace to yourself and others as you smile.

FIRST 30 DAZE · FIRST 30 DAZE · FIRST 30 DAZE · FIRST 30 DAZE

BY

Larry

Day 2: Application

 Go to three places of business today. In many countries, it is normal to say "hello" when you enter a store or place of business, and it also is appropriate in most places to say "goodbye" or "see you later," even if you do not buy anything. In this assignment, feel free to make a purchase, but make it your intention to smile at the people you encounter and say "hello" in your new language. A greeting may be all you can say, but give it a shot. Even if you can only smile at this point, it communicates something positive.

 Write down the responses of the people in the three locations. Did they smile back? Were they helpful? Did you make a new friend?Pray that they may seek Him and find Him.

FIRST 30 DAZE • FIRST 30 DAZE

DAY# ___2___

┌JOURNAL┐

Who did you meet?

What did you eat?

Where did you visit?

Did you learn anything new about the culture?

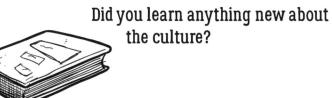

Did you have any language or cultural mishaps?

TAKE A FEW MINUTES TO WRITE DOWN
SOME TAKEAWAYS FROM YOUR DAY.

JOURNAL ENTRY
DAY 2 · 2 · DAY 2
JOURNAL ENTRY

Day 3: Language

"And I am sure of this, that he who began a good work in you will bring it to completion at the day of Jesus Christ."

Philippians 1:6

Day 3: Language

Communication is critical. It is linked to "community" and "commune," a means to share with and connect with others.

Have you ever been in a situation where you could not understand the language around you? How did you feel? The effects may surprise you. You can feel confused, frustrated, stressed, sad, and at times, even angry. You want to understand and be understood, a basic human need. Instead of feeling defeated and disconnected, the goal of connecting can be a motivator to work hard at learning language.

Discover what your style of learning is and jump in. The key is to take risks and speak. It's scary, uncomfortable, and even embarrassing at times, but talking is the only way to acquire a new language. Start with "hello" and use it constantly. It's OK if you can't go past the basic greeting. One of the greatest words of advice I received was to take joy in the little victories. This advice got me through my first weeks of learning. Be happy when you greet someone, knowing that you are making small strides in your ability to speak and reach out to others. Once you manage the basic greeting, get another phrase under your belt and use it. You can't conquer a language in a day.

Some days you will feel like you can speak and other days, you can't say anything. This dilemma is language learning. Don't give up.

One time I taught an adult English-as-a-Second-Language (ESL) class, and one of my Japanese students, a young mom, struggled not only with language, but also with being homesick. She felt worthless, because she couldn't speak English. She felt unloved, because she wasn't with anyone who cared about her. I asked, "Can you speak Japanese?" She looked at me funny (actually more like I was crazy!) and said, "Yes, of course!" I replied, "Speak to me in Japanese. Say anything you want. Just talk to me in your language." She spoke—and then wept. It had been a long time since she had spoken in her heart language to anyone face to face. I said, "You speak the language beautifully. You are capable. You are a smart woman. Don't let anyone tell you differently." Speaking in her own language made her feel worthy again.

Based upon my own experience, language learning is hard. It can make you feel inept, but you aren't. You can endure by the strength Christ gives. Keep on learning and using it. When your confidence wanes, temptation to doubt will come. Your ability to speak another language doesn't define who you are. Your identity is secure in who you are in Christ. It is Christ who completes you, not what you do.

> ## The key is to take risks and speak.

The benefit of language learning is to understand and build relationship with others. When you focus on God instead of self, the motivation to communicate with others changes from pride to service. Language learning is proof that you value the people of your new host culture, which says a lot to those observing you. A friend of mine commented once that language learning is a sign of deference and humility. The less pressure put on yourself to be perfect, the better you will do. It's OK to make mistakes. It is far better to speak a language incorrectly than not speak it at all. Waiting until you are fluent won't make you fluent. Your blunders are opportunities to empathize with other language learners. You will be better equipped to love others well and understand their struggles.

Welcome to a broader worldview. And that's worth celebrating!

Day 3: Application

 Write down (on note cards or in your smartphone) several good phrases you can practice this week. Use them as much as possible. Come up with questions you can ask such as: "Where is the store?" and "Where is the closest subway?" It doesn't matter if you already know the answer; the goal is to practice speaking. Celebrate a language victory for the day!

 Choose one or both of the following language learning ideas to start today:

The language route—Come up with a route around your neighborhood/town in which you can visit certain people to receive language help. Ask each person if they are willing to help you learn the language by talking with you for a few minutes several times a week. Ask for help with the basics: greetings and basic phrases or vocabulary. You can talk about things in the store or about their businesses—whatever they may be willing to talk about. In many cases, they will be workers in a shop or store owners, but it might be repeat customers and clients who frequent the same cafe or store. It also could include a neighbor. Some days they may be too busy. But don't give up; go to the next place.

Label everything or almost—Attach a sticky note to most everything in your apartment with its name in the new language. I promise that you will increase your vocabulary quickly. Maybe try one room at a time so that it's not overwhelming. Enjoy!

FIRST 30 DAZE • FIRST 30 DAZE • FIRST 30

DAY# **3**

⌐JOURNAL⌐

Who did you meet?

_____

What did you eat?

_____

Where did you visit?

_____

Did you learn anything new about the culture?

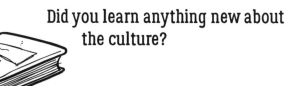

_____

Did you have any language or cultural mishaps?

TAKE A FEW MINUTES TO WRITE DOWN
SOME TAKEAWAYS FROM YOUR DAY.

JOURNAL ENTRY
DAY 3
3

Day 4: Disconnect

"So, being affectionately desirous of you, we were ready to share with you not only the gospel of God but also our own selves, because you had become very dear to us."

1 Thessalonians 2:8

Day 4: Disconnect

"Leaning in" is a phrase often used as we worked with people living abroad. It means to move forward into a new place and culture rather than pining for the home culture. Leaning in takes time and will not happen in the first 30 days. This new way of thinking does not mean you won't or shouldn't be homesick. Most likely you will. We were!

How can one "lean into" the new culture? We moved overseas for the first time in 2001. Those were pre-Facebook, Twitter, Periscope, iMessage, or FaceTime days. We did not even have access to Skype, since it was founded in 2003.

We did have e-mail, but Internet was unreliable. We could call on a land line or send cards and letters (of which I am still a big fan today; nothing like getting a real card, letter, or care package from a friend or family member).

> Connecting to your new culture is beneficial for sharing the love of Christ.

Jim Elliot once wrote, "Wherever you are, be all there! Live to the hilt every situation you believe to be the will of God." I realize it is impossible to disconnect totally from your old culture, but I have found that if you do not disconnect to a certain degree, it is harder for you to "be all there." We know from our experiences if we stay more connected to our home culture than our host culture, we will never make our new place home.

Connecting to your new culture is beneficial for sharing the love of Christ. It is through connecting that you begin to have a heart and passion for the community. First

Thessalonians 2:8 is true. Your new friends will become very dear to you as you interact with and know them more each day.

I remember visiting an expat family in their apartment. They had clocks on the wall set to the times of where their family lived in the States. It looked like a newsroom. Sure, those clocks helped them keep up with the time zones of their children, but perhaps it was a distraction. It would have been for me.

I am not trying to be a social-media killjoy. It is a lot of fun to post pictures for your friends and family and also to see what they post. And it's important for children to connect with family and friends back home. Just make sure there is a balance.

Paul gives an example to follow in 1 Thessalonians—to share yourself with those in your new culture and to hold affection for the people you are among. To be like Paul, you connect with your new home.

Day 4: Application

 Your first assignment today is to be offline and disconnected from your home culture and family. Use some of this free time to pray for the people you've met in your new culture.

 Write down five things you really like about your new home. It can be anything. For example, most businesses shut down on Sundays in Europe, which increased our family time.

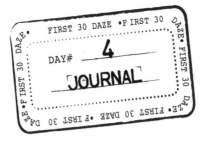

FIRST 30 DAZE • FIRST 30 DAZE

DAY# __4__

⌐JOURNAL⌐

Who did you meet?

What did you eat?

Where did you visit?

Did you learn anything new about the culture?

Did you have any language or cultural mishaps?

TAKE A FEW MINUTES TO WRITE DOWN
SOME TAKEAWAYS FROM YOUR DAY.

JOURNAL ENTRY · DAY 4 · DAY 4 · JOURNAL ENTRY

4

Day 5: Adapting to your new culture

"... I have become all things to all people, that by all means I might save some. I do it all for the sake of the gospel, that I may share with them in its blessings."

1 Corinthians 9:22-23

Day 5: Adapting to your new culture

Understanding the host culture is an important part of thriving overseas. This goal is not attained in a week or month and in some cases, it can take several years. I like the process that my friend and fellow co-author, Caleb Crider, explains in the book, *Tradecraft*. Caleb states that we need to learn cultural exegesis in order to properly understand the new culture around us. Exegesis means to "draw out." Applied to culture, it means gaining understanding from the culture in which you find yourself. We often have a tendency to take our own home culture and simply transplant it into our lives in a new city, thus never fully understanding the new place.

There are several ways you can go about cultural exegesis. You can find ways to learn face to face from people living in the new place. You shouldn't solely rely on what is read on the Internet. You need to ask people questions about their customs, beliefs, predominant religions, food, and values. Basically, you need to understand how they live their lives. When you focus on learning their culture, it shows that you value them and their opinions.

> ...culture shock is inevitable. Identify it early on so you can move past the stress it can cause.

A good example of cultural differences is one we learned during our time in Europe. Americans often "live to work," in which work becomes very high on our value and priority list. However, in Europe, many people we've met "work to live." They value work and want to do well, but work doesn't drive their lives. They desire to have a good and enjoyable life. Cultural differences such as work, food, and customs actually can be shocking. If you have not hit what is called culture shock, you will no doubt at some point. It can be subtle or can sneak up and smack you right in the face. Merriam-Webster defines culture shock as "a feeling of confusion, doubt, or nervousness caused by being in a place (such as a foreign country) that is very different from what you are used to."

We lived almost 15 years in Europe. Many people think living there is like living in the United States. It has similarities, but often there is a veneer of the familiar. After the tourist feeling wears off, reality hits, revealing that you are not in Kansas anymore. In some cases, moving to a culture that is extremely different from your home culture will help you deal with culture shock sooner, because you expect culture shock. Regardless, culture shock is inevitable. Identify it early on so you can move past the stress it can cause.

In 1 Corinthians 9, Paul adapts to the culture in which he finds himself. Why does he do it? For the sake of the gospel. Adapting to your culture goes a long way with others who are watching you. This behavior shows that you care and perhaps one day, you may have the opportunity to share the gospel with them.

Day 5: Application

 Sociologists have a type of field research called "participant observation." It is a technique of field research in which the observer studies the life of a group of people by sharing in its activities. The idea is to find several places of high traffic areas for people. Today, go to at least two gathering spots of the city. Write observations on your phone, or a Moleskine journal (free advertising), and watch people. Observe what they wear, who they are with, their behaviors, and what they are carrying.

 Collect one or more local newspapers and take note of the host culture by looking at advertisements. (In larger cities, free newspapers may be available at public transportation stops.)

 Watch the local news and programs. You can learn what is important to the society from news and entertainment. You may not understand everything, but you will hear the language. You may be able to program some channels to add sub-titles to help you in language learning.

For further reading on adapting to culture:
From Foreign to Familiar by Sarah A. Lanier
Tradecraft: For the Church on Mission by Crider, McCrary, Calfee, Stephens
Ministering Cross-Culturally by Sherwood G. Lingenfelter and Marvin K. Mayers

DAY# **5**

JOURNAL

Who did you meet?

What did you eat?

Where did you visit?

Did you learn anything new about the culture?

Did you have any language or cultural mishaps?

TAKE A FEW MINUTES TO WRITE DOWN
SOME TAKEAWAYS FROM YOUR DAY.

DAY 5 · JOURNAL ENTRY
5
DAY 5 · JOURNAL ENTRY

DAY# ___**6**___

PRAYER

Day 6: Prayer

"And when you pray, do not heap up empty phrases as the Gentiles do, for they think that they will be heard for their many words. Do not be like them, for your Father knows what you need before you ask him. Pray then like this: 'Our Father in heaven, hallowed be your name. Your kingdom come, your will be done, on earth as it is in heaven. Give us this day our daily bread, and forgive us our debts, as we also have forgiven our debtors. And lead us not into temptation, but deliver us from evil.'"

Matthew 6:7-13

Day 6: Prayer

You may be wondering why it took six days to get to the topic of prayer. Well, I assume you've been praying harder than ever in your life and need no reminder! Moving abroad certainly improved my prayer life! There probably has not been a spiritual discipline that has changed so much in the course of my life as prayer. There are days that I flat line; I am without words, feelings, or thoughts that make any sense, so my prayers feel meaningless, even though they are not. There are days I am in a groove, and my prayers have form, order, and meaning. Then there are days that my soul pours itself out before God with such utter dependency and raw emotion that I am spent when finished. Such can be the course of conversation in your relationship with your heavenly Father.

I used to worry that I was not a disciplined Christian, because I didn't always feel "together." But I am learning to embrace the ebb and flow of spiritual conversations. What I realized when I moved overseas was that the most important aspect of my prayer life was not what type of prayer day I was having, but that I was continually in conversation with God.

In 1 Thessalonians 5:17, Paul wrote to the believers in Thessalonica, "Pray without ceasing." Wherever your day takes you, allow prayer to be a continuous thought process, whether on the bus, in a store, walking around the city, or in your home. Reliance on the Lord for each step of the day becomes a certain reality when you truly don't know what each step is going to look like.

Interestingly enough, sometimes it takes getting completely out of my comfort zone in order to rely on the Lord throughout the day. Being uncomfortable shows me the state of my relationship with God. Is it like an "as needed" dosage? When pain is felt, then ask for help? This mentality isn't a relationship with God. Actually, human relationships don't work well this way, either. It's impossible to know someone and grow in relationship if the relationship isn't nurtured. The same is true with God. I used to wait until a special quiet time hour in my day, which is nice to have, but it didn't always materialize. Living in a new city, our schedule was quite sporadic and crazy those first weeks. Praying continually, however, means that you are in communion all day long.

> It's impossible to know someone and grow in relationship if the relationship isn't nurtured.

The impact of being in a continual attitude of prayer changes the way you view the day and the people around you. Culture shock isn't as severe, since you begin to see everything with a more Christ-like perspective. This world is His world, His people; His beauty is all around. Your attitude about your circumstances will change as you walk with Him each step of the way.

49

Day 6: Application

 Write out a prayer to God as if you were writing Him a letter. Update God on what's going on with you, including today. Tell Him the highs and lows of your week. Ask Him for His help on something that has been difficult. Thank Him for all He has done for you and the many ways He is with you. Then end with how excited you are to talk with Him tomorrow.

For further reading:
Too Busy Not To Pray by Bill Hybels
Celebration of Discipline: The Path to Spiritual Growth by Richard J. Foster

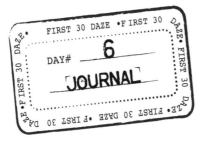

Who did you meet?

What did you eat?

Where did you visit?

Did you learn anything new about
the culture?

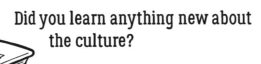

Did you have any language or
cultural mishaps?

TAKE A FEW MINUTES TO WRITE DOWN
SOME TAKEAWAYS FROM YOUR DAY.

JOURNAL ENTRY
DAY 6
6
DAY 6
JOURNAL ENTRY

Day 7: Obedience

"You shall walk after the LORD your God and fear him and keep his commandments and obey his voice, and you shall serve him and hold fast to him."

Deuteronomy 13:4

Day 7: Obedience

Back in 1998 when Larry told me that he felt that God was calling us to go overseas, I was reluctant. My first concern was my children. What would this mean for them? I told him that I would "pray about praying about it" and see what happened. The idea of moving overseas scared me. But true to my word, I prayed and asked God to show me exactly what to do and how it might affect our family. Deciding to pray about this matter was a huge spiritual turning point as I wrestled with what was God's best for us, even if it was not what I had envisioned.

There are several pivotal verses that helped me. In Hebrews 11:8, Abraham also faced the unknown: "By faith Abraham obeyed when he was called to go out to a place that he was to receive as an inheritance. And he went out, not knowing where he was going." He obeyed the Lord and stepped out in faith. Like us, he didn't know where he was going and didn't have a clear plan. But he knew the Lord would provide.

> God calls me to be obedient. Am I willing?

Mary also had to step out in faith. When the angel appeared to her and rocked her world, she answered, "Behold, I am the servant of the Lord; let it be to me according to your word" (Luke 1:38). She humbly acknowledged herself as the Lord's servant and wanted to be obedient, no matter what.

In Matthew 4, Jesus called His disciples. He said in verse 19, "Follow me, and I will make you fishers of men." These men immediately left their nets and families and followed Him. The word "immediately" stands out. They did not wait for further instructions or for time to get things in order. They followed.

As I read through these and other verses in the Bible, I noticed the theme of obedience. God calls me to be obedient. Am I willing? I didn't feel ready for this huge transition overseas, but I was willing to follow God's plan for my life. I had to step out in faith and obey. I prayed that God would show me how to be obedient, and Larry and I began to make plans to move overseas.

It didn't mean that I wasn't afraid. I was completely out of control of the situation and couldn't foresee the future. We seldom have the benefit of seeing around the corner in life. I wanted assurance that all would be well, but instead I received something greater—assurance that He is enough. He can be relied upon.

Having wrestled with these feelings of doubt and fear and coming to a point of obedience not only helped me with making our decision, but it gave me something to remember when things got tough. His love and goodness are evident when we struggle. This time in my life became a spiritual marker, just like the pillars of stones that the Israelites built to remind themselves of what God had done for them along their journey. It is interesting that in Joshua 4:21-24, the same stones that the people of Israel piled were a reminder for the next generation, just as my marker also would be a reminder of God's faithfulness when I could share with my children what He had done. This move wasn't just about me; it was God's plan for my children, too. Fear wasn't completely absent, but I could look back and know that God has been with me and my family all along the way.

FIRST 30 DAZE • FIRST 30 DAZE • FIRST 30 DAZE • FIRST 30 DAZE

BY *Susan*

Day 7: Application

 Fill in the timeline below and indicate any personal spiritual markers when God clearly showed you something He wanted you to learn or do. Write down what you learned from each marker.

BIRTH   **PRESENT**

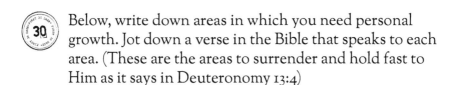

 Below, write down areas in which you need personal growth. Jot down a verse in the Bible that speaks to each area. (These are the areas to surrender and hold fast to Him as it says in Deuteronomy 13:4)

For further reading:
If You Want to Walk on Water, You've Got to Get Out of the Boat by John Ortberg

DAY# **7**

JOURNAL

Who did you meet?

What did you eat?

Where did you visit?

**Did you learn anything new about
the culture?**

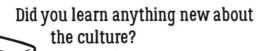

**Did you have any language or
cultural mishaps?**

TAKE A FEW MINUTES TO WRITE DOWN
SOME TAKEAWAYS FROM YOUR DAY.

JOURNAL ENTRY
7
DAY 7 · JOURNAL ENTRY · DAY 7

Day 8: Intentionality

"The heart of man plans his way, but the LORD establishes his steps."

Proverbs 16:9

Day 8: Intentionality

Hitting the ground running can be daunting in a new environment. You don't know much about the new city. As much as reading about a city beforehand helps, it doesn't completely prepare you for being on the ground. The plane lands. You gather your luggage. You head to the first place to sleep. And when I say first place, it might be the first of many! When we moved to Madrid, we slept in six places in four months before finding our own apartment.

You also will have many things on your to-do list these first days. Figuring out transportation needs, where and what to eat, where to register for residency with the government, the new job, kids' schooling, and phone and Internet service are just a few things consuming your first 30 days. (See the *First daze checklist* in back of book for helpful hints.) Did I mention jet lag? How in the world can you be intentional during this crazy time?

Intentionality for me is about getting outside my four walls. Let me explain. Overwhelmed by the newness when we first arrived, I navigated through busy streets, tried to read signs, listened to an unfamiliar language spoken around me and to me (and even possibly about me!), and tried to help my kids adjust. All this took quite a bit of energy. The easy solution was to retreat to my quiet, calm, familiar apartment. As an extrovert, I didn't understand the shift in my personality that made me want to become a homebody! When I say I had to make myself intentionally stay out and engage with my environment, this was my reality those first few weeks, if not months.

Finally, I realized that this tendency to retreat had to stop. I went out the door that morning with a list of places to find in my neighborhood. It became a treasure hunt and was actually quite fun. This effort reaped great dividends and little by little, I found myself feeling more at home.

Intentionality is a mindset. It is saying, "Today I will pay attention to all that is around me. I will engage with others. I will be present." Being fully invested and fully present moves you more quickly from what is new to what is familiar. Intentionality is the ability to determine how you will view your day and how you will engage well. Please note that this has nothing at all to do with being in control. Chances are high you won't be. But God is in control—you don't have to be. Intentionality is waking up and saying, "God, this is your day, not mine. These are your people around me, not mine. I am yours. Whatever you have for me today, I want to be involved." Allow God to establish your steps and guide you in His direction.

> Being fully invested and fully present moves you more quickly from what is new to what is familiar.

There is an expectancy with which you can live each day watching and waiting to see what He will have you observe and do. It is crucial to cultivate an expectant heart in these early days abroad. Being intentional means fighting the "deer-in-headlights" feeling of being paralyzed by newness. It is overwhelming, but living abroad doesn't have to immobilize you. You can determine to view the day as an opportunity to serve and learn from God.

Day 8: Application

 Looking back, write down some activities you accomplished this week. Make note of how each activity became or could become an opportunity. As you step out the door tomorrow, have an expectant heart for God to guide you to seek ways to engage.

Activity	Opportunity
Example: went to grocery store to buy food	made a point to introduce myself to the cashier
Example: dropped kids off at school	next time could stay afterward to meet other parents
Example: found the nearest pharmacy	asked one of my neighbors which pharmacy she uses

For a more logistical oriented to-do list, see the *First daze checklist* in the back of the book.

FIRST 30 DAZE • FIRST 30 DAZE

DAY# **3**

⌐JOURNAL⌐

FIRST 30 DAZE • FIRST 30

Who did you meet?

What did you eat?

Where did you visit?

Did you learn anything new about the culture?

Did you have any language or cultural mishaps?

TAKE A FEW MINUTES TO WRITE DOWN
SOME TAKEAWAYS FROM YOUR DAY.

JOURNAL ENTRY · DAY 8 · 8 · DAY 8 · JOURNAL ENTRY

FIRST 30 DAZE • FIRST 30 DAZE

DAY# 9

LEARNER

Day 9: Be a learner

"So Paul, standing in the midst of the Areopagus, said:
'Men of Athens, I perceive that in every way you are very
religious. For as I passed along and observed the objects of
your worship, I found also an altar with this inscription,
'To the unknown god.' What therefore you worship as
unknown, this I proclaim to you.'"

Acts 17:22-23

Day 9: Be a learner

When I was growing up, I heard a saying that nobody likes a "know-it-all," a person who believes he or she has all the answers. As you live in a new culture, keep in mind that you don't have the cultural knowledge of the people who have lived there all of their lives. We found that some Europeans assume that Americans are arrogant and proud. Americans do tend to be individualistic and have a "pull-yourself-up-by-your-boot-straps" mentality. It's true that as a whole, we are conditioned with statements like, "You can do it," "You are strong," and "If you want something done right, do it yourself!"

Sure, it's good to be prepared, informed, confident, and intelligent about a situation. But if you can't be humble enough to accept that you have a lot to learn from the people around you, it will be much harder to adjust to your new culture.

> Walk away from technology, and walk toward the culture so that you can build relationships.

There was a guy who came to work with us in Spain, a marketplace professional who majored in Spanish and was boastful about it. We chuckled to ourselves, knowing that classroom Spanish is a lot different than day-in and day-out using the language without relying on English. It didn't take long before reality hit him hard, because it is an entirely different animal to be immersed. Classroom teaching is predictable and at the pace of the learner; real-life immersion is not.

A big mental shift must take place to move to another culture. I realized that I did not know everything. I had to learn to be OK with that. I had to have a learner mentality.

When you have a desire to learn from others, it goes a long way in making new friends. Asking questions and listening show respect that you care enough to learn about them and their culture, creating a huge bridge to relationships.

Paul observed and learned about the customs and culture before speaking to those he encountered on his various journeys. He found a commonality, a difference, or even a quote from a poet (Acts 17:28) in the culture to start conversation.

Asking questions or making an observation is a great conversation starter. Yes, I know you can Google or ask your smartphone most anything to get answers, but resist the urge. Walk away from technology, and walk toward the culture so that you can build relationships.

Day 9: Application

 Write five questions below to ask people in your new community. Then go out and ask! Don't ask only one person per question; ask several different people each question. Make note of different or similar responses.

1.

2.

3.

4.

5.

Responses:

FIRST 30 DAZE •FIRST 30 DAZE• •FIRST 30 DAZE• FIRST 30 •FIRST 30 DAZE• •FIRST 30 DAZE• FIRST 30

DAY# **9**

⌐JOURNAL⌐

Who did you meet?

What did you eat?

Where did you visit?

Did you learn anything new about the culture?

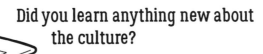

Did you have any language or cultural mishaps?

TAKE A FEW MINUTES TO WRITE DOWN
SOME TAKEAWAYS FROM YOUR DAY.

JOURNAL ENTRY
DAY 9 · DAY 9
9
JOURNAL ENTRY

Day 10: Initiating conversation

"Let your speech always be gracious, seasoned with salt, so that you may know how you ought to answer each person."

Colossians 4:6

Day 10: Initiating conversation

An important part of being a Christ follower is being a representative of Jesus Christ. We are not only representatives through good deeds or actions, but we are ambassadors in our conversations as well. Not every conversation will turn into a spiritual one; in most cases, it takes getting deeper into discussion to get to spiritual matters.

Looking back, I think I did well with greetings and basic sentences, but I could have done much better if I had asked questions and started conversations at a deeper level. I call this the "second question." An example of a "first question" is a basic greeting such as, "How are you?" The second question is something that keeps the conversation going. In many ways, what is said next will determine if the conversation goes deeper. Most people from a variety of cultures will respond to questions unless asked something too personal. If you can learn the skill of asking questions and embrace the awkwardness of being the initiator of a conversation, it becomes easier to get to know others.

The people who do well in cross-cultural communication and adaptation are those who initiate. This behavior is not natural for all of us. It isn't for me. I find that I can be bold enough at times, but other times I shy away. It takes practice not to be afraid to start a conversation.

Our children attended the national public school, and Susan volunteered so that she could be acquainted with the staff and other parents. Little did she know that parents in Spain don't volunteer at schools like in the States. Surprised but needing the help, the teacher invited Susan and a few other mothers to chaperone at the swimming class held at the local community center. As they waited for the children, the teacher and the Spanish mothers asked Susan why she wanted to spend time with them instead of with other American expats in the American Women's Club. Realizing that they assumed all foreigners wanted to be with friends from their own culture, Susan assured them of her desire to have Spanish friends. One lady spoke up and said, "I will be your first Spanish friend." And that is exactly what she became. She showed Susan around town, taught her how to shop at grocery stores, and instructed her in cooking authentic Spanish meals. She also invited Susan and our son to go to the park where many families gathered to play.

> The people who do well in cross-cultural communication and adaptation are those who initiate.

Your willingness to step outside of your circle of home-culture friends in order to befriend your national neighbors will bring a blessing of friendships. Additionally, the host culture and language become more familiar as you are accepted into the community.

Jesus went out of His way to meet people, surprising several with His willingness to speak with them. The Samaritan woman at the well is one whom Jesus approached and initiated conversation (John 4:7-42). He asked her for a drink of water, which led to a conversation about living water. Jesus knew her need for a Savior and offered her new life in Him, the Messiah. His conversations changed lives—an example we can follow as we reach out to spread the gospel.

FIRST 30 DAZE BY Larry

Day 10: Application

 If you are like us, we did not know the language when we moved to Spain or Germany. We worked hard to get down the basic greetings. We didn't want to look foolish, so fear often kept us from continuing the conversation in those early days. Today, go out and simply start a conversation with a neighbor, store owner, or someone on public transportation. Start with what you know in the host language, trying not to use English unless necessary. Make a list of questions below that you would like to ask a person you meet. Write the translation in the host language underneath.

 Once you return, record what happened below. Pray that they may seek Him and find Him.

 What would you do differently?

DAY# **10**

JOURNAL

Who did you meet?

_____

What did you eat?

_____

Where did you visit?

_____

Did you learn anything new about the culture?

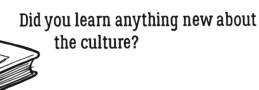

_____

Did you have any language or cultural mishaps?

TAKE A FEW MINUTES TO WRITE DOWN
SOME TAKEAWAYS FROM YOUR DAY.

JOURNAL ENTRY · DAY 10
10
JOURNAL ENTRY · DAY 10

Day 11: Be needy

"And if a son of peace is there, your peace will rest upon him. But if not, it will return to you. And remain in the same house, eating and drinking what they provide, for the laborer deserves his wages. Do not go from house to house."

Luke 10:6-7

Day 11: Be needy

Luke 10 is one of my favorite passages in Scripture. Jesus sends His disciples to a place where He is about to go. He gives them specific instructions and tells them what to expect. Additionally, Jesus mentions a person of peace. This person is one who welcomes and receives you into the community and introduces you to others. He or she also is the person who wants to help you.

As I listened to a Bible teacher speak on Luke 10 one time, he requested that we consider exactly what Jesus asked His disciples to do. Did Jesus indicate to the disciples that it is OK to be needy? Yes! He instructed them to eat what the hosts provided, because they had nothing and were totally dependent on the provision of those whom they encountered.

> Put yourself in the position of the needy one. You need their help!

When problems arise in expat communities or in a study-abroad program, there often is a built-in network for where to go or whom to contact. We can call or text our logistics person for help, but I would suggest starting local. Consider asking a national first. Put yourself in the position of the needy one. You need their help!

Not the most common illustration, but one time I wanted to go fly fishing in Spain. I had no idea where to go or where to purchase supplies. I asked several people and believe it or not, there was one place that sold fly fishing equipment. For those of you who know geography, Madrid is not known for many rivers and lakes in the city. I went to the store and asked the employee, "How does one go about fly fishing inside or outside of the city?" I needed help! After several rounds of trying to explain to him what I needed, he gave me a great contact of a guide who could take me fishing. I did it!

To be honest, reaching out for the help of a local person may totally disarm him or her. It did this man! Most people from other countries think Americans are self-reliant. Prove them wrong—be needy! You may be amazed at the open doors of conversation you will find when you posture yourself in this manner. This neediness can deepen relationships as you show that you need them, and it will help you grow in their culture.

Jesus' disciples accepted the hospitality shown to them by a person of peace. This person has the ability to invite you into his or her community. The only way to find your person of peace is to look for him or her. Look for the person who is eager to assist you and accept the help and friendship.

Day 11: Application

A few days ago, you smiled at and greeted people. Today, think of something you need or you want to find out about in your new city and answer the following questions below:

 What do you need help with? Write it down below and then go find a person to help you.

 What was their response?

 What did you learn about yourself?

For further reading about the person of peace:
Tradecraft: For the Church on Mission by Crider, McCrary, Calfee, and Stephens

FIRST 30 DAZE • FIRST 30 DAZE

DAY# **11**

JOURNAL

Who did you meet?

What did you eat?

Where did you visit?

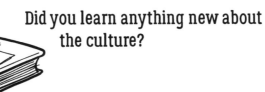

Did you learn anything new about
the culture?

Did you have any language or
cultural mishaps?

TAKE A FEW MINUTES TO WRITE DOWN
SOME TAKEAWAYS FROM YOUR DAY.

JOURNAL ENTRY · DAY 11
11
JOURNAL ENTRY · DAY 11

Day 12: Have fun

"A glad heart makes a cheerful face, but by sorrow of heart the spirit is crushed."

Proverbs 15:13

Day 12: Have fun

Have fun. Now who wouldn't want a piece of advice like this? We all want to enjoy ourselves. So what makes us get so caught up in our lives that we forget to have fun along the way? Life is intense and can be stressful—especially when a big life change is made.

When we moved overseas, we were so intent on doing it right that sometimes we forgot to relax and enjoy the journey. To others, I can only imagine that we looked quite serious! It wasn't long before we realized that fun events needed to be in our schedule. (Yes, you need to put fun on your calendar!) Funny enough, one of the most enjoyable outings for our young children was to go to McDonald's. While in the States, we didn't think of this as a big deal. But overseas, the popular chain became a touch of home. Who knew that a Big Mac could bring joy!

We also loved going to local parks. With a picnic and a Frisbee, we hung out together as a family. Pizza and movie night became a tradition for our family and can also work well for at-home date night or friends' night. You don't have to spend a lot of money to have fun. But you do have to put away work and chores and unplug from social media. Undistracted quality time with family and friends goes a long way in staying emotionally, socially, spiritually, mentally, and physically healthy.

One of the things our children liked to do was watch the street mimes. Frozen in position, a mime didn't move until a coin dropped into a hat on the ground. Once the coin jingled as it landed on other coins, the mime moved about or danced to entertain the audience. This creative show fascinated our son. He quickly deposited all his coins, giving one to each mime we passed. Later when we stopped at a restaurant to eat, I noticed that our son was not present at the table. I looked around and not seeing him, I rushed out of the restaurant. And there was our son—frozen in position with his little baseball cap on the ground. I don't know if he was trying to replace the coins that he spent earlier or loved the idea of entertaining! We laughed and laughed at his entrepreneurial spirit and boldness. He certainly joined the culture around him.

> It wasn't long before we realized that fun events needed to be in our schedule.

Life is busy. I understand. Life goes by quickly, too. But you need to incorporate fun into your life. Take time to enjoy your family and friends. Having a glad heart is a better way to live.

Day 12: Application

 Plan a "fun day." Plan where, when, what, and with whom below. Write it on your calendar and do not cancel.

FUN DAY

date: ....

place: ....

friends: ....

activity: ....

....

prep: ....

....

FIRST 30 DAZE • FIRST 30 DAZE
DAY# **12**
⌐JOURNAL⌐

Who did you meet?

What did you eat?

Where did you visit?

Did you learn anything new about
    the culture?

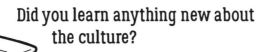

Did you have any language or
cultural mishaps?

TAKE A FEW MINUTES TO WRITE DOWN
SOME TAKEAWAYS FROM YOUR DAY.

JOURNAL ENTRY
DAY 12
12
DAY 12
JOURNAL ENTRY

FIRST 30 DAZE • FIRST 30 DAZE • FIRST 30 DAZE • FIRST 30 DAZE • FIRST 30

DAY# __13__

RHYTHM

Day 13: Rhythm of life

"Therefore do not be anxious, saying, 'What shall we eat?'
or 'What shall we drink?' or 'What shall we wear?' For
the Gentiles seek after all these things, and your heavenly
Father knows that you need them all. But seek first the
kingdom of God and his righteousness, and all these
things will be added to you. Therefore do not be anxious
about tomorrow, for tomorrow will be anxious for itself.
Sufficient for the day is its own trouble."

Matthew 6:31-34

Day 13: Rhythm of life

In our busy culture, we seem to prefer having a schedule. We are creatures of habit and like a routine. What happens when your routine gets interrupted? Are feathers ruffled? Moving abroad dishevels feathers! In my first days, I felt like a chicken in a wind tunnel. Nothing went according to plan. You can plan all day and still be surprised.

If you are a person who lives by a check-off list by the hour, the first 30 days of living abroad will be a test of your patience. There is nothing wrong with planning, but you may have to make adjustments—hopefully with a smile! As you adapt to your host culture, give yourself the freedom to find a new rhythm of life. Look at it as an opportunity to try something new. The more you can view daily life as an adventure to enjoy, the better off you will be. Flexibility in your schedule allows for spontaneous hangouts and pleasant, unexpected coffee dates. Allow time for encountering others and joining in with their activities and lives. Relationally, you will be richer for it.

> The sooner you have friendships, the sooner you will feel at "home."

Not understanding the night schedule of Spain our first few weeks there, we picked up our kids from school, got homework accomplished, ate supper at the American hour of 6 p.m., and then went out as a family to play. To our surprise, there weren't any kids playing at that time. We began to notice that children played outside until 8 p.m., did their homework after that, and ate supper at 9:30 p.m.! When in Rome, do as the Romans do. So we turned our evening schedule upside down so that we could meet people in our neighborhood. Once we adjusted, we enjoyed the late suppers and nights of our new culture.

As you seek the rhythm for your life that fits your new culture, you can discover what God has planned for you in this place. Ask, "Today, how can I seek God's will in all that I do? Am I seeking His kingdom and His righteousness?" Surrender the control of each day to Him.

The sooner you have friendships, the sooner you will feel at "home." Establishing a home is not only important for your kids, but also for you. Find your new rhythm of life and go with the flow. Don't be anxious, because you can trust Jesus to be with you.

Day 13: Application

 Write below a typical week in your new culture. Include waking up/going to bed, work hours, school hours, times of meals as well as where (home or out), leisure time and where (home or out), religious observances (day/times of worship), and other normal things in your schedule.

 To the best of your knowledge, create a new schedule that reflects the typical schedule of your host culture. (Give yourself time to adjust. It may not happen overnight, but gradually you will begin to adapt and enjoy your new rhythm of life.)

 On a yearly calendar, make note of the holidays/festivals of your new culture. You will want to participate somehow in these events. This information is helpful in knowing when businesses, schools, and some public transportation may be closed or have shorter hours.

DAY# **13**

⌐JOURNAL⌐

Who did you meet?

What did you eat?

Where did you visit?

Did you learn anything new about
the culture?

Did you have any language or
cultural mishaps?

TAKE A FEW MINUTES TO WRITE DOWN
SOME TAKEAWAYS FROM YOUR DAY.

JOURNAL ENTRY · DAY 13
13
DAY 13 · JOURNAL ENTRY

Day 14: Eat like a local

"Whenever you enter a town and they receive you, eat what is set before you."

Luke 10:8

Day 14: Eat like a local

I must admit—I love food! And I love eating local food—most of the time. Living in Europe, we had the advantage of good local cuisine. Both Spain and Germany have great food options, and it is easy to find some favorites.

Our most desired local dish in Spain is a breakfast dish called *pan con tomate*. It is a toasted baguette with olive oil, crushed fresh tomatoes, and salt. It sounds simple, but it is amazing. And the perfect pairing is *cafe con leche*, which is strong, smooth Spanish coffee with milk. The tangy, fresh tomatoes with aromatic extra-virgin olive oil grown in Spain, enjoyed with a hot beverage of bold, rich coffee, is perfection!

Not every experience is perfect. For example, knowing the language helps to order meat products, especially since most countries outside of the United States eat every part of the animal! We asked a waiter in our early days in Europe to bring us several dishes that he recommended since we couldn't read the menu. He brought a black sausage that was strange tasting and not very appealing. We looked up the Spanish word when we returned home and found out it was a blood sausage.

Even buying meat at the market can be interesting. I bought what said *hamburguesa* on the package, thinking it was hamburger meat. Yet while cooking, it turned white in color and smelled funny. I pulled the package out of the trash can and with dictionary in hand, I looked up the ingredients. Was I surprised when I discovered that ostrich was to be our main course! With a little ketchup, we ate it. Eating local, depending on where you live, can be a challenge. In our cross-cultural training, we were told that there are food items that our brain is programmed to say, "Not food!" It is hard to convince the brain otherwise, but we really try hard to eat what is set before us, especially if dining in a national's home. We have eaten cow cheeks and rice blackened with squid ink, both very tasty. Sometimes it's better not to listen to these cues from your brain so that you don't taste through a preconceived idea about food. And we don't want to offend a host who has worked hard to prepare a special meal, possibly with great financial sacrifice. Jesus told His disciples to eat the food placed before them by their hosts. He knew how important it would be to show gratitude when taking the message of the gospel to others.

When traveling to an unfamiliar location, we look for the local restaurants. This habit does not mean we avoid sneaking in a meal at an American or internationally-known chain restaurant every once in a while.

> ...we really try hard to eat what is set before us, especially if dining in a national's home.

Eating local, however, is advantageous for several reasons. First, it is generally cheaper to eat local food and shop local markets. I like that a lot! Second, you meet local people and avoid tourists. Third, you observe your host culture. Food is a big part of culture. Observe what people eat or order. Ask questions at the market or in a restaurant. Most places are proud of their local food. We found that in every country that we lived or visited, most people are willing to tell you about the different foods and what is best. You could be offered the chance to test some products out for free. I have been handed a variety of things to pop into my mouth. Most of the time, it has been delicious! Fourth, a new twist in your own cooking is possible. You will gain new recipes to use and insights into cuisine. When you return for a visit to your home culture, you can impress your family with an international dish. They will love trying new foods and hearing your stories, which helps to build a bridge between your two worlds.

FIRST 30 DAZE
BY
Larry

Day 14: Application

Choose one of the following to do today:

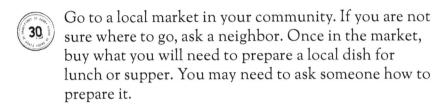 Go to a local market in your community. If you are not sure where to go, ask a neighbor. Once in the market, buy what you will need to prepare a local dish for lunch or supper. You may need to ask someone how to prepare it.

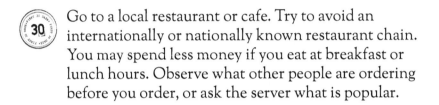 Go to a local restaurant or cafe. Try to avoid an internationally or nationally known restaurant chain. You may spend less money if you eat at breakfast or lunch hours. Observe what other people are ordering before you order, or ask the server what is popular.

FIRST 30 DAZE • FIRST 30 DAZE • FIRST 30

DAY# **14**

⌐JOURNAL¬

Who did you meet?

What did you eat?

Where did you visit?

Did you learn anything new about
the culture?

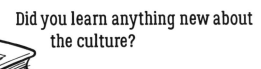

Did you have any language or
cultural mishaps?

TAKE A FEW MINUTES TO WRITE DOWN
SOME TAKEAWAYS FROM YOUR DAY.

JOURNAL ENTRY
DAY 14
14
DAY 14
JOURNAL ENTRY

Day 15: Shop like a local

"And when Jesus came to the place, he looked up and said to him, 'Zacchaeus, hurry and come down, for I must stay at your house today.' So he hurried and came down and received him joyfully."

Luke 19:5-6

Day 15: Shop like a local

There's nothing better than a guide book that instructs you to shop! But I might add that this includes "window shopping." (Sorry, avid shoppers.) No matter which shopping you do, both can be fun and informative. To get out, walk around, and go into shops, even the ones you wouldn't normally go into, are important steps in your first 30 days.

Observe the products, the clients, the shop owners, and employees. Go to food markets, even the smelly fish ones. Frequent pharmacies, post offices, office supply stores, furniture stores, fruit stands, antique galleries, second-hand shops, art galleries, and definitely bookstores. Shop at the businesses near where you live. All are windows into your host culture—past, present, and probably future, too.

> You honor them by taking interest in their work and lives.

What does it mean for those in your neighborhood that you are willing to come into their places of business to see what they sell or eat in their restaurant? You honor them by taking interest in their work and lives. There is a shop near the apartment where we lived that Larry frequented often. Because the owner and my husband both have a love for coffee, they built a close relationship over the years. It all started when his friend and he decided that they each needed to practice language. He wanted to learn more English, and Larry needed help with Spanish. Once a week, they met for coffee and for conversation in each other's language. Their topics were varied, and often they asked questions. One conversation concerned his negative view toward the church and religion. My husband shared about the difference between religion, which can be a list of rules, to focusing on what it means to have a personal relationship with Jesus, the One who died on the cross for us. Not only has Larry found a lifelong friend, but we have seen this man grow closer to an understanding of God's love for him.

We also befriended a lady at a local grocery store in Germany and made a point to speak to her each time we shopped. Our conversations were quick since she was working, but it led to us asking more about each other's lives. Soon we were stopping on the street to chat when we saw her. It was wonderful to see how a friendship could develop from a smile and kind words in the midst of everyday errands.

I don't know much about Jesus' shopping habits, but He made a point of greeting people and spending time with them, even if they were not favored. Jesus honored Zacchaeus by making the effort to come to him and visit him in his home. Zacchaeus' response was one of joy, and the visit made such a difference in his life that he turned aside from his deceitful ways and decided to follow Jesus. Find ways to honor those around you in your new culture.

Day 15: Application

 Today, I want you to actually buy something within your budget. (Do not buy a couch and tell yourself it is for a cultural learning exercise. That's not on me!) Perhaps you might purchase clothing of your host culture so that you fit in a little better, like an accessory, a shirt, or a pair of shoes. In Spain, everyone wears a scarf in the winter. Even my language teacher told me that I would get sick if I didn't wear a scarf to cover my neck. Regardless of its germ defying powers, I did realize that a scarf was a simple, inexpensive way to begin to fit in. If you don't want to buy an article of clothing, buy something small to decorate your apartment or to cook with that fits the culture. It's amazing how wearing or displaying in your apartment something from your host country makes you feel at home.

FIRST 30 DAZE • FIRST 30 DAZE

DAY# __15__

⌐JOURNAL⌐

Who did you meet?

What did you eat?

Where did you visit?

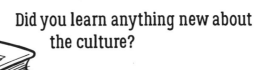

Did you learn anything new about
the culture?

Did you have any language or
cultural mishaps?

TAKE A FEW MINUTES TO WRITE DOWN
SOME TAKEAWAYS FROM YOUR DAY.

JOURNAL ENTRY
DAY 15
15
DAY 15
JOURNAL ENTRY

Day 16: Gathering spots

"So he reasoned in the synagogue with the Jews and the devout persons, and in the marketplace every day with those who happened to be there."

Acts 17:17

Day 16: Gathering spots

The Apostle Paul had a knack for finding out where people met so that he could meet them in their space. In various places in the New Testament, he goes where the Jewish people gather for prayer. He starts conversation and is noticed. He also goes to the marketplace. As a tentmaker, Paul knows the business lingo. He enters into locations where people are and hangs out.

Hanging out in gathering spots is a great way to learn your new city. One way to find these spots is to purchase or find a free map of the city or area. You even can draw your neighborhood and mark the gathering spots on the map. I always am amazed that some restaurants and cafes have no customers while others are extremely crowded. The crowded ones usually are your gathering spots for the locals.

You will want to observe the times people gather. It was mentioned on a prior day to find the rhythm of the city. As you learn when people go to work, take coffee breaks, eat lunch, and hang out after work, then you can map out your gathering spots.

> Finding where people gather is a key to meeting people and eventually sharing the gospel.

There is a local gourmet market in Madrid that not only is a historical site, but it is where people shop and eat on Saturdays from 11 a.m. to 3 p.m. Individual vendors sell their goods in the market, such as fresh seafood, meats, and vegetables. Delicious food is served as well, so people enjoy standing around eating and talking. We usually met some of our friends at this market and found ourselves in multiple conversations with others, learning about the people who lived in our neighborhood by running into them there. Our social circles grew, and we felt more connected with the existing social community. Some great conversations came as a result as we talked about hopes, disappointments, and joys in our lives.

Jesus in the midst of a crowd is common in God's Word. He knew where people gathered, whether that was in the synagogue, on the town streets, by the sea, or on a hillside. He looked at the crowds with compassion. They needed physical healing but most importantly, spiritual healing. And that's what you are to do—see the crowds before you with the compassionate eyes of Jesus so that you can give them hope through Jesus Christ.

Finding where people gather is a key to meeting people and eventually sharing the gospel. Who knows whom you might share your faith with over *churros* and chocolate?

Day 16: Application

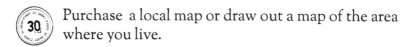 Purchase a local map or draw out a map of the area where you live.

With your map in hand, walk around your neighborhood or community and mark where people meet.

Finally today, enter a gathering spot. Order a drink or food and observe what happens around you. Determine how you may be able to connect with people there. Ask the Lord to give you a person you can talk with while you are there.

Check to see if your city has a version of www.meetup. com where you can find existing groups to join or you can start your own. You also can find out a lot about your neighborhood by reading the local newspaper.

FIRST 30 DAZE

DAY# **16**

⌐JOURNAL⌐

Who did you meet?

_____

What did you eat?

_____

Where did you visit?

_____

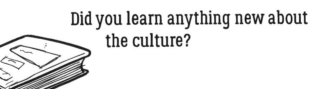

Did you learn anything new about
the culture?

_____

Did you have any language or
cultural mishaps?

TAKE A FEW MINUTES TO WRITE DOWN
SOME TAKEAWAYS FROM YOUR DAY.

JOURNAL ENTRY
16
DAY 16
DAY 16
JOURNAL ENTRY

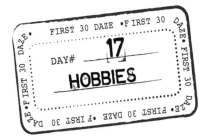

Day 17: Don't lose your hobbies

"This is the day that the LORD has made; let us rejoice and be glad in it."

Psalm 118:24

Day 17: Don't lose your hobbies

Hobbies can be erratic. Sometimes we have them, sometimes we don't, for one reason or another. Most of the time, they just change as we change, get older, or have new priorities. What makes us choose what we do for relaxation anyway? Do we watch others enjoy a hobby and decide we want to pick it up? Or does a personality type or family tradition determine our choices? No matter what hobbies we have, medical advice would tell us not to work all the time but to relax as well. One of the first things dropped when going through a big change, especially if it is a stressful one, is leisure time activities.

> Having a common hobby with others leads to friendships and connections you might not have otherwise.

There are three reasons for pushing pleasurable activities to the side when moving abroad. First, we lose a normal schedule. We become too busy surviving and adjusting that we can't fit in anything else. Second, we are tired. It takes a lot of physical and mental energy to adjust to a new culture. I came home from language school exhausted mentally and physically. I didn't understand how I was so worn out from verb conjugations! What little energy left was used to make dinner, do a load of laundry, or help the kids with homework. There was no time for a jog. And third, the setting changes. If you love to relax by fishing, chances are there is no access to a fishing spot in proximity to a big city. Or if a cyclist lives in an area with no safe roads or trails, a bike can't be ridden easily. All of these factors make holding on to hobbies a bit tricky.

Truth be told, you need a hobby now more than ever. The best thing I could have done after a day of language school was to go on that jog, even if I didn't feel like it. Permitting yourself to rest and relax is key to being able to have longevity. You might have to choose another hobby that is more suitable for where you live now. Or it might be fun to choose a popular hobby of the local culture. One hobby we picked up was coffee roasting. Because we enjoy specialty coffees, everywhere we go we visit a coffee shop. As we became regular customers at coffee shops, we often engaged in conversation with owners about roasting. Hobbies that give open doors to spiritual conversations are worth trying. Whatever you choose, make it a regular part of your life so that you can unwind and build relationships in the process.

Recreation is good for you on many levels. It is refreshing to the soul to step away from work and have down time. A hobby helps maintain good health, physically and mentally. Having a common hobby with others leads to friendships and connections you might not have otherwise. God intends for you to enjoy the day He has given you.

When our family lived in Germany, hiking became a love for us. Sunday afternoons turned into a time for family hikes on one of the many trails where we lived. Not only did these regular outings bond us as a family, but we truly relaxed in the great outdoors with countless other Germans who did the same.

My husband quotes a statement that has stuck with me on all of our many moves: "We are running a marathon, not a sprint." In other words, we need balance. We can't go full steam ahead all the time and not rest. Even Jesus took time away from the crowds when necessary. If we continue on full blast, that lifestyle will lead to burnout or failure. Scheduling time for a hobby will bring sanity to your schedule and a sense of well-being.

Day 17: Application

 Make a list of your hobbies, past and present, then add any hobby that you have an interest in but have never done. Circle one hobby on the list that fits with your new lifestyle and culture and put it on your schedule.

FIRST 30 DAZE • FIRST 30 DAZE

DAY# **17**

[JOURNAL]

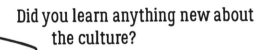

Who did you meet?

What did you eat?

Where did you visit?

Did you learn anything new about
the culture?

Did you have any language or
cultural mishaps?

TAKE A FEW MINUTES TO WRITE DOWN
SOME TAKEAWAYS FROM YOUR DAY.

JOURNAL ENTRY · DAY 17 · 17

Day 18: Join a local group

"And on the Sabbath day we went outside the gate to the riverside, where we supposed there was a place of prayer, and we sat down and spoke to the women who had come together."

Acts 16:13

Day 18: Join a local group

You have moved to a new place and still may not know one person in your city. That is completely normal. You may have a few colleagues at your school or place of employment, but other than that, you are starting from zero. As scary as it is, do not fear. Before long, you may have several local or international friends.

In the cities where we lived, we found that many people participate in clubs. It may be the local football club (soccer), language-learning class, tennis club, art class, or book-reading group. A few years ago, I heard about a coffee-making class at a local coffee shop. My son and I signed up and learned what a barista does—the best part being the free coffee we sampled! Who wouldn't enjoy that? Another time while in Stockholm, Sweden, we walked through a park and saw a huge outdoor yoga class. What a great way to meet others in the neighborhood!

Find a place that you can join. It will help you connect to your new community and will help you feel invested in the local culture. You will meet new people who may become your best friends overseas.

Joining a gym or fitness facility is another great way not only to meet others, but to stay in shape. It is amazing how many CrossFit places are opening up all over the world. Getting plugged into your community will lead to opportunities to share your faith. Incorporating your hobby with a group of others with the same interest is a great way to be a part of an existing group.

The Apostle Paul often made his practice to join prayer gatherings or go to a place of prayer. In Philippi, Paul and his companions went to the riverside and saw a group of women gathered for prayer. These women believed in God but did not know the gospel of Jesus. A woman name Lydia happened to be there. God opened her heart to hear Paul's message. She and her family believed and were baptized. Then she begged Paul to stay with her family.

> You will meet new people who may become your best friends overseas.

Joining a group will give you a chance to meet people of various religious beliefs. You will learn much about their culture, faith, and values. Natural conversations occur in groups of people with a common interest as others get to know you and as you know them.

Day 18: Application

 You may be able to find out about local clubs on www. meetup.com. This is not an endorsement of the website but a source. Below, write down any existing clubs you are aware of that interest you or clubs that you want to find. Asking people and doing a Google search are two more ways to find existing clubs. Another source may be a bulletin board of community events at your language school.

FIRST 30 DAZE • FIRST 30 DAZE • FIRST 30

DAY# **13**

⌐JOURNAL⌐

Who did you meet?

What did you eat?

Where did you visit?

Did you learn anything new about
the culture?

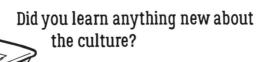

Did you have any language or
cultural mishaps?

TAKE A FEW MINUTES TO WRITE DOWN
SOME TAKEAWAYS FROM YOUR DAY.

JOURNAL ENTRY
13
DAY 18

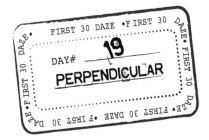

Day 19: Perpendicular pathways

"and also for me, that words may be given to me in opening my mouth boldly to proclaim the mystery of the gospel, for which I am an ambassador in chains, that I may declare it boldly, as I ought to speak."

Ephesians 6:19-20

Day 19: Perpendicular pathways

I love the story in Acts 8:26-40 in which Philip is instructed by the Lord to go south on the desert road. It may not have made a lot of sense to him at the moment, but he listens to the Lord. As he goes southward on the road, he sees an Ethiopian official sitting in his chariot while he reads. God's Spirit impresses Philip to go over and join the man, and Philip again obeys. As he approaches, he hears the man reading the book of Isaiah. He asks the Ethiopian if he understands what he's reading. The Ethiopian official invites him into the chariot to ride along as he explains the Scriptures to him. Philip didn't have to invite himself! Philip is able to explain the gospel of Jesus, the Lamb of God who was foretold by the prophet Isaiah. The Ethiopian becomes a believer in Christ and is baptized in water by the road.

> ..."divine appointment"—an encounter and opportunity occurs, completely arranged by God.

This incident is a great example of one man who obeyed the Spirit's leading to meet a person whom God put on his pathway. In this case, it was a onetime conversation between Philip and the Ethiopian. This type of encounter is a perpendicular pathway—when we unexpectedly cross over into someone's life whom we may never see again. Some call this a "divine appointment"—an encounter and opportunity occurs, completely arranged by God.

Ask the Lord to give you divine appointments. I spent time in a city in the Middle East. It was actually my first time there and due to some bad weather, I was snowed in. (I couldn't believe it snowed in the Middle East!) All of my appointments were cancelled for the day because of the weather and not being able to travel on the roads. I decided that I did not want to stay in my hotel room, so I ventured out to walk in the neighborhood where I was staying. Before leaving my room, I read Luke 10 several times about Jesus sending out the 70 disciples. I prayed that God would bring about a divine appointment and direct me to people who could speak English, Spanish, or German, since I did not know Arabic. I had several things written down if I got into a conversation. God answered my prayers and led me to a few people who spoke English. I was not able to share the whole gospel with them, but I knew that God had put those people in my pathway. I trusted that the seeds planted could be built upon in the future.

God arranges perpendicular pathways. You have to ask for them, look for them, and listen to God's Spirit when He urges you to do something. But you can't leave it at that. You have to be bold enough to obey God and do what He tells you to do.

Day 19: Application

 Pray for a perpendicular pathway to encounter a person in your neighborhood or city.

 Prepare by identifying the area where you want to start out, writing down your abbreviated and brief testimony in the host language (will be very basic) and thinking through some stories of the Bible you have memorized in English, in case you meet someone who can understand English.

 Go into your community, praying and watching as you walk.

 Write down what happened below.

DAY# 19

JOURNAL

Who did you meet?

What did you eat?

Where did you visit?

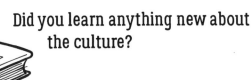

Did you learn anything new about
the culture?

Did you have any language or
cultural mishaps?

TAKE A FEW MINUTES TO WRITE DOWN
SOME TAKEAWAYS FROM YOUR DAY.

JOURNAL ENTRY
DAY 19
19
DAY 19
JOURNAL ENTRY

Day 20: Parallel pathways

"and what you have heard from me in the presence of many witnesses entrust to faithful men who will be able to teach others also."

2 Timothy 2:2

Day 20: Parallel pathways

In Matthew 4:18-20, Jesus calls His first disciples: "While walking by the Sea of Galilee, he saw two brothers, Simon (who is called Peter) and Andrew his brother, casting a net into the sea, for they were fishermen. And he said to them, 'Follow me, and I will make you fishers of men.' Immediately they left their nets and followed him."

Jesus simply invites these two fishermen to "follow Him." The theme of obedience is once again evident in these two brothers who drop their nets and follow Jesus. They spend three years being discipled by Him as they minister alongside. An on-going personal relationship develops as Jesus the disciple-maker prepares them to disciple others.

When God brings people to come along beside us, it is called parallel pathways. In many cases when we plant ourselves in a new city, we look for opportunities to share our faith and/or mentor others in the faith. In some cases, these are perpendicular encounters as mentioned on Day 19, but in most cases, people whom we see frequently, if not daily, in our normal routines are referred to as parallel pathways.

We recently moved from a city that we love dearly. On our last day there, we decided to personally say goodbye to the shop owners and workers whom God allowed us to build relationships with while living there. It was amazing to realize how many people we interacted with on a day-to-day basis. This is what it means to live parallel with so many people.

How do you talk and interact with the people who live parallel with you? How do you share the gospel or mentor them to become more mature followers of Jesus? You can start by identifying them, making note of where you encounter them, what you have in common, what you know about them, and any other pertinent information concerning where they stand on spiritual issues. Then you make the effort to be intentional to meet up with them and spend time together.

There was a woman in our community whom we met, and once we got to know her, we found out that she had a son who needed a tutor. Susan became the son's tutor in their home, which led to seeing the family on a regular basis. This contact brought about opportunities to share our faith.

> When God brings people to come along beside us, it is called parallel pathways.

Jesus went out to find His disciples. He approached them. Most likely, it will begin with you to seek and discover these parallel people whom God has entrusted to you.

Day 20: Application

 Make a list of people in your area whom you have met. It may only be one or two people, but write them down. Then make a list of the places you frequent.

People whom I have met:

Places I frequent:

 Make a point this week to interact with the people you've met and go by the places that you frequent. Start praying for opportunities to interact with these parallel people on a regular basis and be intentional to start connecting. You may be surprised by the doors the Lord opens for you as you live out your faith as salt and light in your neighborhood.

DAY# **20**

[JOURNAL]

Who did you meet?

What did you eat?

Where did you visit?

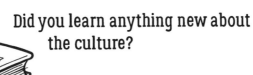

Did you learn anything new about the culture?

Did you have any language or cultural mishaps?

TAKE A FEW MINUTES TO WRITE DOWN
SOME TAKEAWAYS FROM YOUR DAY.

JOURNAL ENTRY · DAY 20 · JOURNAL ENTRY · DAY 20 ·
20

Day 21: Looking beyond yourself

"... Truly, I say to you, as you did it to one of the least of these my brothers, you did it to me."

Matthew 25:40

Day 21: Looking beyond yourself

One of the biggest challenges in a transitional phase of life is not becoming too self-focused. Of course, you do need to be aware of how you are adapting and taking care of yourself, but the tendency is to assess everything by how it affects you. Part of this inclination has to do with our natural instinct to survive and be protected from any outside threat or harm. Being in a new environment does make us react more cautiously. In fact, the impact of the environment can be subtle enough that we don't even realize that the focus is on ourselves.

> Simple ways to serve speak loudly.

A servant attitude will draw you out of self-absorption mode. A simple act of kindness goes a long way in showing how you care about others in your community. Greet those you encounter as you are moving about the community each day. As your language skills improve, ask a neighbor how he or she is doing, or possibly what he or she is doing today. Hold a door open for someone. Assist a neighbor struggling with her groceries. Let someone go in front of you in the checkout line. Simple ways to serve speak loudly.

When we first moved to Spain, my language skills were deficient. I was eager to make friends, but other than using hand gestures, it was hard to communicate. I decided to make brownies to take to my neighbors so that I could introduce myself and at least say hello. It wasn't until later when I could speak Spanish and became friends with many of them that I heard how this initial act of kindness impacted them. We always refer to that time as our "brownie ministry," and this gesture helped bond us with our neighbors.

Another act of kindness is to befriend the regulars on your street who may solely survive on playing music or demonstrating another artistic talent rather than begging. By listening to them and putting a little money in a cup esteems their ability to sustain themselves without begging. It also gives you the opportunity to make friends. There was a homeless woman on the corner of our street who sold small items such as tissue or umbrellas. I made a point to purchase something from her in order to help her self-employment be sustainable. It gave me an opportunity to talk with her, too. Sometimes I brought her coffee or a pastry. I eventually was able to have spiritual conversations with her. She even found me a church to attend!

As well as reaching out to individuals, find ways to volunteer in community organizations in your city. Volunteer to help with a clothing or food distribution center. Sign up to serve in a food kitchen or work in a kid's club. Make food for an ill neighbor or someone who recently had a baby. Take cookies to your neighbors or invite them for tea or coffee. Stepping outside of your world and entering into someone else's world increases your capacity to serve and love well. A servant lives out the gospel in a tangible way. Your needs become less of an issue when you focus on how to cause someone else to smile.

Day 21: Application

 List some of the ways or places where you have served in your home culture.

 Brainstorm and write down a few possibilities of how you might serve a neighbor today and in the future.

 Research some places or organizations in your new city where you can serve. Make appointments to check out these places and prayerfully consider them. List below.

 Several cities around the world have a network organization like "Serve the City" (servethecity.net). See if your city has one of these networks. They match volunteers with projects.

DAY# **21**

[JOURNAL]

Who did you meet?

What did you eat?

Where did you visit?

Did you learn anything new about
the culture?

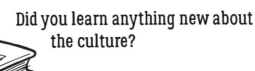

Did you have any language or
cultural mishaps?

TAKE A FEW MINUTES TO WRITE DOWN
SOME TAKEAWAYS FROM YOUR DAY.

JOURNAL ENTRY · DAY 21 · JOURNAL ENTRY · DAY 21

21

Day 22: Hospitality

"Show hospitality to one another without grumbling."

1 Peter 4:9

Day 22: Hospitality

Hospitality is an act of kindness that used to be daunting to me. I grew up in the South where hospitality is a natural part of the culture. There is certain etiquette to be followed in the South—setting the perfect table, cooking the flawless meal, welcoming guests into your clean home, and drawing your guests into conversation are all a part of a fine art called Southern hospitality. It truly is beautiful to watch someone who is a gracious hostess. Knowing I would never match up to the perfect hostess, however, made me nervous about inviting people over. I didn't want to be judged by my lack of skill in pulling off the ideal meal or event.

Over time, I began to realize that hospitality isn't about a table setting or food. Hospitality is making people feel comfortable in your home. It can be stressful to host people in your home if you put pressure on yourself to have everything just right. It also can deter you from inviting anyone over. There is a time for an elegant evening, but there are more opportunities for casual get-togethers.

I love having people in my home. It is fun to welcome guests and friends and to spend time in the comfort of a living room instead of a restaurant. Eventually, I learned not to worry about the presentation but instead concentrated on loving and serving my guests.

Just as I overcame the fear of not being the perfect hostess, I also had to overcome the fear of making cultural mistakes when entertaining in another country. It's important to research cultural taboos, but in the end, people are more gracious than you think when you do make a mistake. You want to be able to serve food that is not offensive to their religious beliefs. You also want to be aware of any gender issues in regard to eating together or separately or shaking the hand of the opposite sex. Ask before they come or ask a friend who can clue you in to cultural norms. Just don't let the unknown stop you from inviting people over! The love you show your guests far outweighs the fancy hors d'oeuvres you serve or mistakes you make.

> Hospitality is making people feel comfortable in your home.

A friend of mine once told me that she invited a Muslim family over for tea. She wasn't ready to ask them over for a meal and wasn't sure if they would accept this early in the relationship anyway. When they arrived, she shook the wife's hand and then reached out to the husband to shake his hand. Immediately, he reacted by moving backward and saying, "It is not proper for a man to touch a woman who is not his wife!" Needless to say, she apologized and never made that mistake again! Over a few months of persistence, the families became close friends, and many opportunities to share the gospel and give a Bible became possible.

Being hospitable and being truthful about your "welcome" mat at the door will make a difference in how you are received into the community. Invite others over and have a good time!

Day 22: Application

 Invite a new friend or neighbor over for a cup of coffee. If it is more comfortable for you, invite him or her out for coffee the first time and then invite to your home the next time. You are probably thinking, "Well, once I have more of the language, I will feel more comfortable." Resist the urge to wait. It can be a short visit. There may be awkward pauses of silence as you struggle for what to say, but relax and allow the person to teach you some new sentences. The point is to make the effort to get to know someone.

 Take the opportunity to get tips from other expats for entertaining in your host culture. Also, when you are invited to someone's home, watch carefully what the hostess does. Watch how she handles the evening, from welcoming to serving to conversing to saying goodbyes. Specific things to watch for include what to do with shoes when entering a house, where people are seated at the table, which room the family eats in, and who helps the hostess wash the dishes.

DAY# **22**

JOURNAL

Who did you meet?

What did you eat?

Where did you visit?

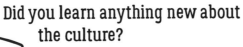

Did you learn anything new about the culture?

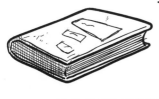

Did you have any language or cultural mishaps?

TAKE A FEW MINUTES TO WRITE DOWN
SOME TAKEAWAYS FROM YOUR DAY.

JOURNAL ENTRY
DAY 22
22
DAY 22
JOURNAL ENTRY

Day 23: Enjoy the honeymoon

"Behold, what I have seen to be good and fitting is to eat and drink and find enjoyment in all the toil with which one toils under the sun the few days of his life that God has given him, for this is his lot. Everyone also to whom God has given wealth and possessions and power to enjoy them, and to accept his lot and rejoice in his toil— this is the gift of God. For he will not much remember the days of his life because God keeps him occupied with joy in his heart."

Ecclesiastes 5:18-20

Day 23: Enjoy the honeymoon

According to Kalervo Oberg, anthropologist, there are phases of cultural adjustment. The "honeymoon" phase is a joyful time of excitement to live in a new place. You embrace this new world, and each day is an adventure. There will be naysayers who say, "Oh, you are just in the honeymoon phase; it will wear off." Don't listen to them. Smile and enjoy your honeymoon.

In the first 30 or more days, you are more motivated to learn, so take advantage of this phase for maximum learning. A friend of mine commented that she is still in the honeymoon stage after years as her love grows for the people and culture. Even as you go through different phases of living abroad, when you are in a place that God has called you to, you can be confident that He will give you the strength to face hard times and to stay. There is nothing wrong with being enamored with the newness of living abroad. This giddiness is an essential piece of cultural acquisition. Falling in love with the new culture is helpful for longevity. It will be good to write down how you feel upon arrival so that you can read it in the future.

> There is nothing wrong with being enamored with the newness of living abroad.

The funny thing is that when you return to your home culture someday, the things that drove you crazy about living abroad will all of a sudden become the things that are most dear. You will remember the things you did, the people you met, the shops you entered, the food you ate, and the language mistakes you made. You will laugh at these special memories with affection.

To this day, our family fondly remembers celebrating a holiday in Spain and Germany called King's Day. Our first King's Day was in the honeymoon phase, so we were eager to observe this holiday on January 6. Many other countries commemorate the gifts that the three kings gave baby Jesus, so they give small gifts on this day. The day before, crowds of people watch a parade featuring the three kings. After the parade, the children place their shoes outside the door before they go to sleep in anticipation of the kings bringing a good gift. They hope they don't receive a lump of coal! Although we exchanged gifts on Christmas Day, our family took up the tradition and also observed gift-giving on King's Day. We even bought a little cake shaped like a crown just as the nationals buy. It was fun to observe a new holiday, which we enjoyed celebrating and still do to this day.

Around this same time in our first days, we learned the tradition of shooting off fireworks on New Year's Eve. It's like the Fourth of July on this night in other parts of the world. We felt like the honeymoon phase of living abroad for us was one big party!

Make many special memories in these first days. You will treasure them for years to come.

Day 23: Application

 Write out two or three things that you love about this new culture.

 Write your first impressions and moments of delight in your new city in a journal every day. These written reminders are fun to review on the days when you need to remind yourself to smile.

FIRST 30 DAZE • FIRST 30 DAZE

DAY# **23**

⌐JOURNAL⌐

Who did you meet?

What did you eat?

Where did you visit?

Did you learn anything new about
the culture?

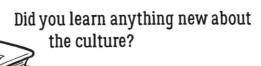

Did you have any language or
cultural mishaps?

TAKE A FEW MINUTES TO WRITE DOWN
SOME TAKEAWAYS FROM YOUR DAY.

Day 24: What to do when you don't feel like doing anything

"If the LORD had not been my help, my soul would soon have lived in the land of silence. When I thought, 'My foot slips,' your steadfast love, O LORD, held me up. When the cares of my heart are many, your consolations cheer my soul."

Psalm 94:17-19

Day 24: What to do when you don't feel like doing anything

Let's be honest. There are some days when you don't feel like doing anything. We all have these days. My friend calls it her "747" days since she feels like getting on a plane and heading home. It may or may not be homesickness causing the doldrums. It might be weariness, discouragement, or fear. Psalm 94:17-19 are some of my favorite verses. They sustain me on days when I am weary and need a lift to my spirit. God carries us through difficult days; we can look to Him to hold us up and cheer our soul. He is there to catch us when we slip into a dark time.

Right before moving overseas, I asked a seasoned veteran of living abroad for his best piece of advice. He thought for a minute and said, "On those days when you don't feel like going out the door, go!" I didn't know how significant this advice would be until the day I needed it.

> ...make yourself get up, get dressed, and go out the door.

In Spain, a Spanish driver's license is needed to drive a car. Larry failed the test about six times! He was so stressed and frustrated about it that he forced himself to accept that the only way our family could travel was to walk, ride a bike, or ride public transportation. We couldn't sit around sulking. So we started to ride bikes everywhere. All went well until one of our children and I came out of a store with a bag of groceries one evening and found that someone had stolen the seat off my bicycle! I had to walk home with groceries, the bike, and our child. Even though losing a bike seat was a small incident, it felt like it was the tipping point for Larry who was frustrated with the results of not having a driver's license. He was ready to buy us plane tickets home! Sometimes it is the small things that push us over the edge. We had to work hard to push through this stressor, but we did with God's help.

There are mornings when you will wake up, and the last thing you want to do is go out the door. Although this feeling can happen anywhere, it seems magnified in a new culture. On days like these, make yourself get up, get dressed, and go out the door. You don't have to go out for long. It might be to walk around the neighborhood or run a few errands. Moving about lessens the feeling that a cloud is hanging over you.

Sometimes, you do need to disengage and rest. But be aware that cultural stress can be overwhelming if you dwell on it rather than deal with it. Facing your reality head on can minimize the dread and give you the boost you need.

Day 24: Application

 Write a letter to yourself on a piece of paper or in your journal. Start the letter with Psalm 94:17-19 and any other verse that encourages you. After that, write one of your most fun experiences since you have been in the new culture. Next, remind yourself of the reasons why you chose to make this big move and why you feel this is where you are supposed to be. Sign your name and date it at the bottom. Then tuck the letter in a safe place for a day in the future when you need encouragement.

DAY# **24**

JOURNAL

Who did you meet?

What did you eat?

Where did you visit?

Did you learn anything new about
the culture?
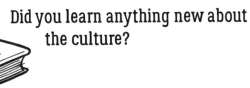

Did you have any language or
cultural mishaps?

TAKE A FEW MINUTES TO WRITE DOWN
SOME TAKEAWAYS FROM YOUR DAY.

JOURNAL ENTRY · DAY 24
24
DAY 24 · JOURNAL ENTRY

Day 25: Emotions

"For God alone, O my soul, wait in silence, for my hope is from him. He only is my rock and my salvation, my fortress; I shall not be shaken. On God rests my salvation and my glory; my mighty rock, my refuge is God. Trust in him at all times, O people; pour out your heart before him; God is a refuge for us."

Psalm 62:5-8

Day 25: Emotions

What makes a move overseas different from a move within your own country? For me, it was overwhelming to adjust to a new way of doing things as well as a new language. I know you may be thinking that, of course, it will be different. However, it won't be only one thing that's unusual to you; it could be that most things are poles apart from your home culture.

> You cannot change the circumstances around you, but you can determine how you will respond.

Some of these new things might include transportation, housing, electricity, water usage, sanitation, greetings, ways of eating, time change, daily schedule, clothing, paperwork, Internet and phone, and on and on. Coupled with not being able to communicate well (even forming a sentence to ask someone how something works or what to do) creates a continual state of stress. You feel tension in the everyday little things that used to be second nature. Functionality is disrupted. You never had to think about how to flush a toilet or where to buy stamps. You shout, "Why can't I do anything like I used to?!"

This state of anxiety manifests itself into a variety of emotions. Who knew that trying to make toast could reduce you to tears or figuring out where to go on the subway would make you spontaneously combust? Be aware of your stress level and recognize that these emotions may not be directed at the subway but more at your ability to function normally. A friend recommends finding the balance between acknowledging how you feel and understanding it but then moving on instead of "camping out" in your emotions. Actually, the way you respond to pressure affects others. If you have a spouse, children, or even a colleague, your attitude can determine how others around you react to their stress.

My children were aware when I was confused and frustrated. I didn't even have to say anything! They picked up on cues of a serious look, nervous posture, or a withdrawn attitude. If I showed anger, it wouldn't be long before I saw one or both of them get angry when frustrated. Those around watch our responses, and before long a domino effect begins. It's normal to have anger, fear, sadness, or concern while trying to adjust to a new culture, but it's important to model a Christ-like response, even admitting to others that it is not always easy. A repentant spirit is a way of living out our faith authentically.

You cannot change the circumstances around you, but you can determine how you will respond. Be gentle with yourself as well as those around you. Realize that your life is going to look differently in a few months and give yourself time to adjust. How can you show yourself some grace? Allow yourself time to relax. You may need to take a walk or read a book. Find ways to unwind so that you can handle what comes next. Take your emotions to the Lord and ask Him to guide you through these challenging days. Read His Word as your source of comfort and encouragement. You may not think it is true now, but in time you will feel better about your ability to handle daily stress. Psalm 30:5b reminds me that "weeping may tarry for the night, but joy comes with the morning." Hang in there!

Day 25: Application

 What are the emotions you have had since arriving in your host culture? Beside each emotion, write down what triggered the emotion and what might be the underlying cause of each feeling.

Emotion	Situation	Underlying Cause
Ex: angry	wrong bus stop	confusion, fear

 Take time to thank God for the place and people He brought you to, and ask Him to help you deal with emotions. Ask Him to show you how to handle the situations that arise in the future. You may want to write down your prayer below.

 Who did you meet?

 What did you eat?

 Where did you visit?

Did you learn anything new about
the culture?

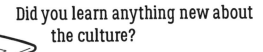

 Did you have any language or
cultural mishaps?

TAKE A FEW MINUTES TO WRITE DOWN
SOME TAKEAWAYS FROM YOUR DAY.

JOURNAL ENTRY
DAY 25
25
DAY 25
JOURNAL ENTRY

Day 26: Kids

"And these words that I command you today shall be on your heart. You shall teach them diligently to your children, and shall talk of them when you sit in your house, and when you walk by the way, and when you lie down, and when you rise."

Deuteronomy 6:6-7

Day 26: Kids

Wait! Don't skip over this day if you don't have kids! We all live life in community so at some point, you will likely interact with a family living overseas or headed that way. The best way to love others well is to understand them better and know what they face. Get to know a family with kids and be a support and encouragement. It can be a breath of fresh air to have family around you.

Oh, kids! What a bundle of fun! There isn't anything quite like viewing a new experience through the eyes of children. They see things we can't. Listen to them. Learn from them. Let them show you what they see, hear, and feel.

We moved overseas with a 6- and a 10-year-old. And we learned a lot from them. I will never forget Larry coming up with the "great idea" that we would all practice our Spanish at the dinner table each night. This began soon after arriving, and none of us were comfortable with the language yet. The first dinner we tried was the quietest dinner ever! Not a word was spoken! (By the way, don't use this as a technique to ensure peaceful dinners!) It didn't take long to realize that our kids needed to connect with us in our heart language. It felt awkward for them to talk to us in this new foreign language. In hindsight, forcing language practice at the dinner table was a mistake. Sensing what your kids need (or don't need) will help them adjust and give them a sense of security.

> Sensing what your kids need (or don't need) will help them adjust and give them a sense of security.

There are three things I tried to do with our children: listen, play, and pray. Listening involves hearing what they say and noticing their actions, attitudes, and emotions. When your child isn't talking, he or she is still communicating! Attentively playing with your children also helps you to know how they are doing. Your relationship with your child becomes richer, more meaningful, and sweeter. I have no basketball skills, but shooting baskets with my children was one of the best ways that I connected with them. Conversations flowed, laughter abounded (mostly at me!), and stress dissolved.

Most importantly, pray with and for your children. Model simple prayers of praise, repentance, intercession, and thanksgiving. As you model conversational prayer, your children will see that they, too, can talk with God continually. Give thanks to the Lord as a family for all that you are learning and experiencing.

Day 26: Application

 If you have children, give them a disposable camera or your smartphone as you walk around the city, and let them take pictures of what they see. This will give you a child's eye view of his or her new home. The photos will make a great scrapbook for them to look back on someday. You also can give them art supplies to paint or draw a picture of what was seen. You might even draw a picture with them and talk about it together. (If you don't have children, ask an expat family if you can tag along with their family one day!)

DAY# __26__

JOURNAL

Who did you meet?

What did you eat?

Where did you visit?

Did you learn anything new about
the culture?

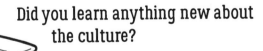

Did you have any language or
cultural mishaps?

TAKE A FEW MINUTES TO WRITE DOWN
SOME TAKEAWAYS FROM YOUR DAY.

JOURNAL ENTRY
DAY 26
26
DAY 26
JOURNAL ENTRY

Day 27: Finding church

"And they devoted themselves to the apostles' teaching and the fellowship, to the breaking of bread and the prayers. And awe came upon every soul, and many wonders and signs were being done through the apostles. And all who believed were together and had all things in common. And they were selling their possessions and belongings and distributing the proceeds to all, as any had need. And day by day, attending the temple together and breaking bread in their homes, they received their food with glad and generous hearts, praising God and having favor with all the people. And the Lord added to their number day by day those who were being saved."

Acts 2:42-47

Day 27: Finding church

Over the years, we watched people who lived abroad struggle to find a community of believers with whom to worship. Often people find themselves in places where there are few Christians. Others find themselves with many options including the expat international church, a national church, or a home-cell church comprised of a few believers.

Three different times, our family lived in a city abroad in Germany and Spain. When we moved to Spain the first time, we desired to be a part of a Spanish-speaking church. After visiting several, we received an invitation by another expat to a church that caught our attention. The people were friendly and welcoming. It was important to us to have a group of believers where we could fit in well and serve, and we connected with them quickly. It also was important that we hear biblically sound teaching. During the time of worship, the Spanish words to the songs were projected on a screen, which helped us participate in the singing right away. Our children thrived among these special people.

After several years, it was time to move our work to another part of the city. Our children's needs changed since they were in national schools, so we attended an international church that literally was made up of internationals from every inhabited continent of the world. We had a glimpse of what it will be like in heaven to be worshipping God with people from every tribe and nation. The services were in English, but other languages were present in songs, prayer, and Bible reading. Our children felt comfortable hearing English and engaged quickly. Our daughter even played in the youth worship band.

Both styles of church bodies fulfilled purposes in our family at different seasons of life. We are grateful that we were a part of two faith communities within our new culture. Involvement in a church body is important for your growth as a believer and gives you community with other believers. There's a real temptation to wait until you're settled to find a community of believers who meet together, but refrain from delaying.

I challenge you to visit a church body as soon as possible. Perhaps by the end of your first 30 days, you will find a church home. Though you may only be in your city a short time, being involved in a local body gives you a place to worship, serve, and fellowship.

What if there are no believers where you live? Worship together as a family or pray about starting a church in your home.

> We had a glimpse of what it will be like in heaven...

Don't forget your church back in your home culture! It also is important to stay connected. You are a sent-out one being salt and light in another land. While you may not consider yourself a full-time vocational missionary, you are an ambassador of Christ. Your home church provides accountability, prayers, and on-going community. (You will find out ways to get your home church involved and connected with you overseas on Day 28.)

Day 27: Application

 If you haven't found a church body yet, research church options you may have in your neighborhood. Visit one of them this week. We recommend that you visit a few and pray through the ones where you feel you can have good community, solid Bible teaching, and be involved. If there are no church options, consider starting a missional community of believers in your home.

For more information on starting a community of believers, see *Everyday Church, Gospel Communities on Mission* by Tim Chester and Steve Timmis.

Who did you meet?

What did you eat?

Where did you visit?

Did you learn anything new about the culture?

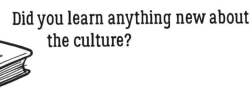

Did you have any language or cultural mishaps?

TAKE A FEW MINUTES TO WRITE DOWN
SOME TAKEAWAYS FROM YOUR DAY.

JOURNAL ENTRY
DAY 27
27
DAY 27
JOURNAL ENTRY

Day 28: Prayer support

"And so, from the day we heard, we have not ceased to pray for you, asking that you may be filled with the knowledge of his will in all spiritual wisdom and understanding, so as to walk in a manner worthy of the Lord, fully pleasing to him, bearing fruit in every good work and increasing in the knowledge of God. May you be strengthened with all power, according to his glorious might, for all endurance and patience with joy, giving thanks to the Father, who has qualified you to share in the inheritance of the saints in light. He has delivered us from the domain of darkness and transferred us to the kingdom of his beloved Son, in whom we have redemption, the forgiveness of sins."

Colossians 1:9-14

Day 28: Prayer support

Asking for prayer support is not reserved only for non-profit service and missions organizations. Today, more and more people who are believers are transferred overseas by employers, even to some countries where religious workers have a hard time securing visas. You don't have to be a "vocational missionary" to be a witness for Christ in another country. But you can learn from the missionary that you need people back home to pray for you.

There are many traditional ways and even more creative ways to communicate with friends, family, and church groups from home who love you and are willing to pray for you and those whom you encounter. Providing a photo prayer card can serve as a daily reminder for people to pray. Posting regular updates on social media or by e-mail gives prayer supporters a look into your daily life and with those you meet who need to hear the good news. You may decide to write a daily blog. Communication apps such as Slack, WhatsApp, WeChat, Evernote, Signal, Line, Instagram, Viber, FaceTime, and many more are beginning to take over the popularity of Skype. Whichever method to communicate you choose to use while you live abroad, it is comforting to know someone is interceding to the Father on your behalf as soon as you send a specific request.

> To know someone is praying for you each day is an encouragement.

You will have many prayer needs in your time abroad. There will be decisions to make, difficulties in your job, temptations you face, and joys to share.

On March 11, 2004, terrorists struck Madrid in several train stations, killing 192 people and injuring around 2,000. We sent an e-mail immediately to our prayer support team to let them know that we were OK and to pray for our national friends who lost friends, family, or co-workers. We also asked them to pray that we could use this opportunity to comfort our neighbors and share the hope Christ gives. As we delivered flowers and a card to all of the families who lived in our building, God answered the prayers of those back home. Our neighbors openly welcomed our efforts to reach out, and deeper spiritual conversations and friendships began.

For many years, I had a group of seven men from my home church who prayed for me while I lived abroad. I asked each one to sign up for a day each week to pray for me specifically. To know someone is praying for you each day is an encouragement. It provided accountability so that I was able to share struggles or victories with friends invested in supporting me this way. I also prayed for these men. The bond between us became strong as we prayed for one another.

It only takes a moment to send a short note home to ask for prayer. People want to pray for you, so don't be afraid to ask.

Day 28: Application

 Think of a few people who can be your prayer advocates. Ask them if they are willing to pray for you on a regular basis. Decide on the best way to communicate.

 Write your first brief post or e-mail. People love bullet points for specific prayer requests. Plan to update your post regularly.

FIRST 30 DAZE • FIRST 30 DAZE • FIRST 30 DAZE • FIRST 30 DAZE • FIRST 30 DAZE

DAY# **28**

⌐JOURNAL⌐

Who did you meet?

What did you eat?

Where did you visit?

Did you learn anything new about
the culture?

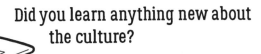

Did you have any language or
cultural mishaps?

TAKE A FEW MINUTES TO WRITE DOWN
SOME TAKEAWAYS FROM YOUR DAY.

JOURNAL ENTRY · DAY 28
28

Day 29: Life as worship

"I appeal to you therefore, brothers, by the mercies of God, to present your bodies as a living sacrifice, holy and acceptable to God, which is your spiritual worship."

Romans 12:1

Day 29: Life as worship

I can remember the day as if it were yesterday. We had been in our new country for about five months and had made a valiant effort of being engaged with the community and settled as a family. We found a local church to be a part of, and although we didn't understand much of what was being said or sung, we were glad to find a place to worship and meet people. This particular day, the apartment needed cleaning. I listened to music as I cleaned, a CD of worship music from our home church in the States. When I heard the familiar words and tunes that spoke to my heart, I broke down and sobbed. It touched a deep part of me found lacking—worship.

A fault of mine exposed itself, one that was present far before this episode. It was strikingly clear that I relied upon my hour at church on Sunday mornings to be my only source of worship. How can one hour of music, a sermon, and fellowship carry me throughout my week? It wasn't that I didn't participate in scheduled quiet times and prayer times, but I honestly didn't view them as worship like I did my church service.

God gently reminded me in that moment that worship is not one hour on Sunday morning. Worship must be continual. All of me, every day. Whether I walk on the streets, greet my neighbors, ride the subway, wait in the long line at the government office for my visa, or spend time with my family. Every single thing I do, say, think, feel, and experience is an opportunity to give Him glory.

When we first moved to Spain, immediately we noticed that most people bought their bread from street vendors or at a bakery instead of the grocery store. Wrapped in paper and still hot, I carried fresh bread home often, sometimes enjoying a bite before getting home! One day as I continued my worship on a morning commute, I bought bread and instantly thought of Matthew 6:11: "Give us this day our daily bread," one part of the prayer Jesus taught His disciples. Jesus is the Bread of Life. God meets all of our needs in Christ, who is our daily bread. He meets our spiritual needs, our physical needs, and our emotional needs. We lack nothing with His provision. But we don't worship Him because of what He provides for us. The God of the universe deserves our worship because of who He is. He is worthy to receive all glory, honor, and praise all the time.

> ...worship is not one hour on Sunday morning. Worship must be continual. All of me, every day.

Why wait for that one hour on Sunday to be in communion with your heavenly Father when He is waiting for you each moment of the day? He is waiting. Go to Him and be in awe of His goodness and grace. And worship Him.

Day 29: Application

 Search your heart and determine how you worship God. How do you give glory to Him in all things?

 Does everything in your day point to Him as your heavenly Father, Savior, and Creator? Take time to pray and commit to worshipping Him daily.

 Who did you meet?

 What did you eat?

 Where did you visit?

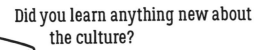 Did you learn anything new about the culture?

 Did you have any language or cultural mishaps?

TAKE A FEW MINUTES TO WRITE DOWN
SOME TAKEAWAYS FROM YOUR DAY.

JOURNAL ENTRY
29
DAY 29

Day 30: Don't take yourself too seriously

"do not be anxious about anything, but in everything by prayer and supplication with thanksgiving let your requests be made known to God. And the peace of God, which surpasses all understanding, will guard your hearts and your minds in Christ Jesus."

Philippians 4:6-7

Day 30: Don't take yourself too seriously

I must admit when we chose the topics for 30 days, I, Larry, had to write this day. Looking back on my first 30 days we lived overseas, I took myself way too seriously! My original goals were lofty. I was going to be the best overseas worker ever.

Language learning was extremely important to me, even though I was not very good. Understanding a cross-cultural setting was proudly my expertise, or so I thought. Sharing my faith was my reachable target, but I was disappointed when it took longer than anticipated to make even a small difference. The results of taking myself so seriously were internal pressure, discouragement, and thoughts of giving up. I nearly drove myself crazy.

> It is OK to mess up and OK to not succeed at everything, because even in failure, He has a purpose.

There's no shame in trying hard, but something happened to me along the way. I forgot that it was OK to mess up. I got really frustrated when I made language mistakes. One time, I was at the post office and asked for four *cuellos* instead of *sellos* for stamps. The post office attendant looked at me and said, "Do you really need four necks?" Instead of laughing with the worker, I got mad at myself and took out my frustration on the man like it was his fault. Talk about first impressions this national acquired about me!

For two years, I struggled with this destructive mindset until God convicted me of my self-absorption. I forgot what it meant to have fun and trust God. He was the One who had set me on this path, and He would be the One to sustain me, direct me, teach me, and draw people to Himself possibly through me. It is OK to mess up and OK to not succeed at everything, because even in failure, He has a purpose. When I began to focus on abiding in Christ and seeking Him to use me for His kingdom purposes, regardless of my ineptness, I began to see improvement in my skills to function in a new culture and my attitude toward my circumstances abroad.

Going way out of my comfort zone so that I could have fun again, I joined a parents' basketball league at our son's school. I thought about joining the soccer club for about a nano-second until I realized that those parents played like professionals! Being an American, however, I was somewhat a star on the basketball court since basketball isn't as popular overseas as soccer. I wasn't that great at playing, but they thought I knew way more than they did! Playing actually built some confidence in me regardless of my language ability, because it gave me a chance to interact, have fun for several hours, and drink coffee with "the team" afterward.

God delights in His people. You have the privilege to glimpse God's love for the world and His desire for all to know Him as you move overseas. He created you to reflect His glory to the nations. When you reflect the Father's glory and imitate Him, a watching world sees God's love for them. Life can be heavy and full of trials. You can easily get caught up in the stress of your move and forget to enjoy God, each other, and life. It may sound cliché, but count your blessings and take joy in what God has done, what He is doing, and what He will do. Be a blessing to those around you by sharing your joy. Mistakes made in a new culture will fade away, but the beauty and majesty of the Lord stands forever. Keeping a heavenly perspective makes the first 30 days an adventure and a treasure to be cherished.

Day 30: Application

 List the things you are taking way too seriously. Consider what things you can't laugh about yet, you don't excel in, or you can't control.

 Spend time in prayer, offering this list to the Father and asking Him to restore your joy and your trust in Him as you move forward in His kingdom purposes.

Who did you meet?

What did you eat?

Where did you visit?

Did you learn anything new about
the culture?

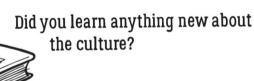

Did you have any language or
cultural mishaps?

TAKE A FEW MINUTES TO WRITE DOWN
SOME TAKEAWAYS FROM YOUR DAY.

JOURNAL ENTRY · DAY 30

30

Afterword

There is no perfect "how to" guide to live abroad intentionally. What works for one person or in one host culture may or may not work for another. Our point of reference is a European culture, but we think you'll find most of these principles applicable. Life can be "on-the-job training," and you will learn about culture in your own unique situation. Learn from others who have been there and who can offer wise advice, and take good notes on the journey so you can pass on tips to others in the future.

We don't claim to have all the answers for the first 30 days you are overseas, but we know that we had countless questions when we moved and imagine you might, too. Having a teachable spirit helped us to learn through our mistakes. Some things came a little easier, because we listened to the advice from friends. The key is to keep learning. If someone can glean at least one thing from our thoughts that helps, especially during the "daze" period, we have accomplished what we set out to do.

We are so grateful to have had the privilege and honor of living abroad and learning to see beyond ourselves. Our worldview is bigger, we have a greater appreciation for things we previously took for granted, we have respect for people who aren't like us, and we have a richer love for others. Last but not least, we have a deeper love for God and His care. For these reasons, and many more, we are thankful for the journey. We pray your journey brings rich dividends, too.

"The LORD bless you and keep you; the LORD make his face to shine upon you and be gracious to you; the LORD lift up his countenance upon you and give you peace" (Numbers 6:24-26).

Larry and Susan McCrary

197

First daze checklist

Here are a few initial things to check off your list upon moving abroad.

☐ Make a map or find a map and mark gathering spots, places you frequent, and things on this list below

☐ Find grocery options and hours

☐ Get cell phones connected or buy minutes

☐ Find out national emergency number (their version of 911)

☐ Find route to nearest hospital or clinic

☐ Introduce yourself to your apartment complex guard/ gatekeeper

☐ Make sure your children have your contact info on them at all times

☐ Practice routes home with the family, including public transportation

☐ Practice transportation routes to frequented places

☐ Find out about taxi rates and routes

☐ Find a 24-hour drugstore in your city

☐ Find ATM machines

☐ Find Wi-Fi spots or set up in your apartment

- [ ] Find local cafes

- [ ] Inquire about local food specialties and try the local cuisine

- [ ] Find a local doctor

- [ ] Find city hall or community center for registration

- [ ] Locate police station

- [ ] Locate American consulate and register as citizen living abroad

- [ ] Find local parks

- [ ] Find local recreation/fitness center

- [ ] Register your children for school

- [ ] Register for classes at a local language school

- [ ] Locate an IKEA or furniture store and inquire about delivery

- [ ] Open account with a local bank

- [ ] Inquire with a neighbor about recycling and trash pickup

- [ ] Find a local movie theater and inquire about a national movie with English subtitles

- [ ] Attend a local perfomance highlighting the culture or history or find a local history museum

- [ ] Find a market where a local specialty is made

About the authors

Larry McCrary is the co-founder and executive director of The Upstream Collective and the founder of The Skybridge Community, an international marketplace network. He is co-author of *Tradecraft* and author of soon-to-be-released *The Market Space.*

Susan McCrary loves teaching English as a Second Language (ESL), being part of an international community, and being involved with refugee ministry. She loves to speak and share about living intentionally and being missional at home and abroad.

Originally from Knoxville, Tennessee, Larry and Susan have been involved in ministry and missions over the past 30 years, both in the U.S. and overseas. They spent the past 15 years mostly living in Europe. They are blessed to have two "third-culture kids" who have shared their journey and brought much joy along the way. Presently, Larry and Susan live in Louisville, Kentucky, leading The Upstream Collective.

Made in the USA
Middletown, DE
15 June 2017